BLOCKING & UNBLOCKING

DON'T PAINT YOURSELF INTO A CORNER

JAMES MARSH STERNBERG MD (DR. J)

authorHOUSE

AuthorHouse™
1663 Liberty Drive
Bloomington, IN 47403
www.authorhouse.com
Phone: 833-262-8899

Published by AuthorHouse 03/01/2021

ISBN: 978-1-6655-1842-0 (sc)
ISBN: 978-1-6655-1841-3 (e)

Library of Congress Control Number: 2021904142

Print information available on the last page.

This book is printed on acid-free paper.

ACKNOWLEDGEMENTS

This book would not have been possible without the help of several friends. Frank Stewart, Michael Lawrence, Anne Lund, and Eddie Kantar all provided suggestions for material for the book.

I am forever indebted to Hall of Famer Fred Hamilton and the late Bernie Chazen, without whose guidance and teaching I could not have achieved whatever success I have had in bridge.

I want to thank my editor Randy Baron for his valuable assistance. Any errors in the books are totally mine.

And of course, I want to thank Vickie Lee Bader, whose love and patience helped guide me thru the many hours of this endeavor.

James Marsh Sternberg MD
Palm Beach Gardens FL

THIS ONE'S FOR

RUTH

&

STEVEN

INTRODUCTION

Many problems arise in the play of the cards due to blocked suits. We have all unfortunately had the experience of finding ourselves stranded in the wrong hand, unable to enjoy the tricks that belong to us. This should only happen to our opponents. A classic example:

A K 8 7 6 4	10 9 3	Declarer must take care to play the 10 and 9 under the A K to avoid ending in the short side. This is called "unblocking."

On defense, suit establishment at times becomes impossible because one defender has allowed himself to be left with a card too high in his partner's suit. The suit is blocked. Defenders should strive to prevent such a situation from happening. A classic example:

	A 8 3		West leads the queen. Whether declarer plays low
Q J 10 6 2		K 5	or not, East must play the king. Otherwise, when
	9 7 4		East wins the king, the suit is blocked.

Unblocking is to avoid being left with a blocking card in your partner's suit, otherwise suit establishment can become impossible to make progress. When this occurs, the suit is said to be blocked.

Searching for extra entries, unblocking can be useful. Consider:

K J 9 3	Extra entries are available in both directions if
A Q 10 5	these are played in the proper sequence.

In this book, we will see a variety of examples of how to unblock your suits and how to block theirs. Mastering these will lessen your frustrations. The plays are easy, it's the anticipation in sufficient time that is a good deal more tricky. I'm sure you will recognize some of these situations from your own times at the tables where you may have found yourself blocked. There is some overlap; some of the hands could belong in more than one chapter.

Learning to unblock, wrote Louis Watson in "Play Of The Hand", is akin to the fellow who paints himself into a corner, or the chap who sits on the outer edge of a limb while sawing it off from the main trunk.

CONTENTS

PART ONE: THE OFFENSE

BASIC

UNBLOCKING

SITUATIONS

BASIC UNBLOCKING SITUATIONS

There are hands when certain methods of play develop during the ordinary course of play where declarer can avoid imposing an extra burden upon oneself in the search for extra tricks. One of the most important of these is unblocking.

A few simple examples:

1. North: A K 8 6 4 2   2. A Q 9 8 3   3. A Q 8 5 4

   South: 10 9 3   K 10 4   K 10 9 7

In # 1, if declarer simply wishes to cash out the suit and plays the A-K from dummy, he must be careful to drop the 10-9 from hand. Otherwise, if the suit is 2-2, he will win the third round in hand and need an extra entry to dummy.

In # 2, a standard safety play is to cash the ace first, then lead back to the king, guarding against J-x-x-x with West. However, declarer must take care to unblock the ten on the first round to have a later finesse position. West will not be so kind as to cover the ten on the third round.

In # 3, declarer cashes the ace first to guard against J-x-x-x in either defender's hand. But he must be careful to unblock the 10. If both follow to the ace, he plays to his king, then leads the nine to the queen. Otherwise, he will be cut off from dummy if either defender holds J-x-x-x.

4. North: A Q 10 5

   South: K J 9 3

In # 4, if declarer needs extra dummy entries, he leads the king to the ace, then the jack to the queen. If both opponents follow, he can play the nine to the ten, the three to the five, four entries. If he needed entries to his hand, he would cash the ace and then have three entries to his hand.

GETTING OUT
OF YOUR
OWN WAY

CAREFUL DECLARER UNBLOCK

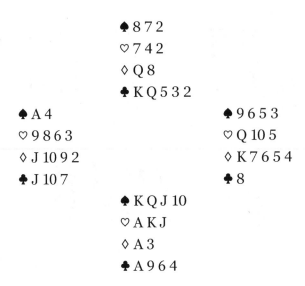

♠ 8 7 2
♡ 7 4 2
◊ Q 8
♣ K Q 5 3 2

♠ A 4
♡ 9 8 6 3
◊ J 10 9 2
♣ J 10 7

♠ 9 6 5 3
♡ Q 10 5
◊ K 7 6 5 4
♣ 8

♠ K Q J 10
♡ A K J
◊ A 3
♣ A 9 6 4

Contract: 3 NT
Opening Lead: ◊ Jack

Declarer hopefully tried the queen from dummy at trick one, but East produced the king. Not good. The opponents were poised to take a lot of diamond tricks. Declarer knew he could not try for any spade tricks. However, with a successful heart finesse there might be nine tricks.

He won the diamond return, cashed the club ace and led low to the club king. He took a successful heart finesse and claimed. The claim was rejected.

Question: Why was the claim rejected? What would you have done differently?

The first declarer had blocked the club suit and was forced to win the fourth club in hand with the nine. The other declarer saw the problem in time. The play started the same, but he led the club nine to dummy's king.

After the successful heart finesse, he had nine tricks. He still had the four of clubs in his hand to unblock the club suit and take five club tricks. Careful play pays off.

UNBLOCKING

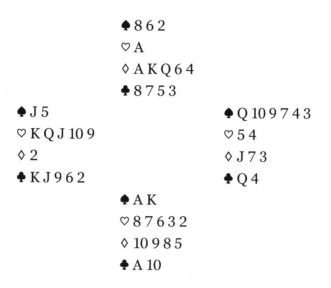

```
                    ♠ 8 6 2
                    ♡ A
                    ◇ A K Q 6 4
                    ♣ 8 7 5 3
    ♠ J 5                              ♠ Q 10 9 7 4 3
    ♡ K Q J 10 9                       ♡ 5 4
    ◇ 2                                ◇ J 7 3
    ♣ K J 9 6 2                        ♣ Q 4
                    ♠ A K
                    ♡ 8 7 6 3 2
                    ◇ 10 9 8 5
                    ♣ A 10
```

Contract: 3 NT
Opening Lead: ♡ King

Declarer counted nine tricks as long as East did not have four diamonds to the jack. When he cashed the diamond ace, he anxiously looked around and was relieved to see everyone follow suit. So relieved that he was a bit careless.

He then claimed nine tricks, announcing, "I'm taking two spades, one heart, five diamonds, and one club." The claim was rejected again.

Question: What now this time? How did he mess up this no-brainer?

The other declarer also was relieved to see everyone follow to the diamond ace, but he had followed with the diamond ten, not the five as did the first declarer who had blocked the suit.

The first declarer took only four diamonds, having to win the fourth diamond in hand. The other declarer unblocked the 10-9-8 under the A-K-Q, then the six in dummy was high. He took five diamond tricks.

TAKING CARE TO UNBLOCK

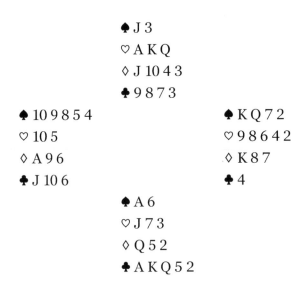

```
                    ♠ J 3
                    ♡ A K Q
                    ◊ J 10 4 3
                    ♣ 9 8 7 3
    ♠ 10 9 8 5 4              ♠ K Q 7 2
    ♡ 10 5                    ♡ 9 8 6 4 2
    ◊ A 9 6                   ◊ K 8 7
    ♣ J 10 6                  ♣ 4
                    ♠ A 6
                    ♡ J 7 3
                    ◊ Q 5 2
                    ♣ A K Q 5 2
```

Contract: 3 NT
Opening Lead: ♠ 10

With the spade lead, there was no time to try to set up the diamonds. Declarer won the ace, cashed the club ace to be sure the clubs were not 4-0, playing low from dummy, and claimed nine tricks.

"I don't think so," said an alert East. "Down one." North's icy stare was enough to melt glass.

Question: Do you see why the claim was rejected?

Declarer had blocked the suit. The other declarer was careful to call for the club nine when he played the ace. And then he unblocked the seven and eight. He took the nine tricks the other declarer was only thinking about.

Of course, it's painful to be defending when a declarer doesn't unblock, the suit divides 2-2 and they escape. Sometimes there is no justice.

UNBLOCKING TO FINESSE

```
                    ♠ 10 4 3
                    ♡ A K 4
                    ◇ J 2
                    ♣ K Q J 7 2
      ♠ 8 7 2                        ♠ J 9 6 5
      ♡ 10 9 6 3                     ♡ Q 8 5
      ◇ K 8                          ◇ A 10 6 5 3
      ♣ A 10 5 4                     ♣ 6
                    ♠ A K Q
                    ♡ J 7 2
                    ◇ Q 9 7 4
                    ♣ 9 8 3
```

Contract: 3 NT
Opening Lead: ♡ 3

Declarer played low and East won the queen. East returned a heart. Declarer came to his hand with a spade and led a club. The king won. He led the club queen, West won, East showed out. West continued with another heart.

Question: Did the above declarer make 3 NT? What is the problem?

At the other table, play started the same. The other declarer also wanted to start the clubs from his hand, to not lead the king and lose to a singleton ace.

He led the club eight to the king, winning. When he continued with the queen, he played the nine. But now, with a small club in hand, he could finesse West who held ♣ 10 5 in front of dummy's ♣ J 7. He took nine tricks.

What club did you have left in your hand? Did you unblock?

UNBLOCKING TO FINESSE LATER

```
                    ♠ A K
                    ♡ Q J 4 2
                    ◊ 10 6 2
                    ♣ K 7 5 2
    ♠ J 10 9 5 4               ♠ Q 8 3
    ♡ A 10 9                   ♡ K 8 6 5
    ◊ 9                        ◊ J 7 5 3
    ♣ Q J 10 4                 ♣ A 6
                    ♠ 7 6 2
                    ♡ 7 3
                    ◊ A K Q 8 4
                    ♣ 9 8 3
```

Contract: 1 NT

Opening Lead: ♠ Jack

Declarer won in dummy and led a diamond to his ace. When he cashed the king, West showed out.

Question: Did declarer make 1 NT? How would you have played?

At the other table, declarer knew if West had four diamonds to the jack, there was nothing he could do. But if East had four, he needed to take care to play the diamond ten on the first round of diamonds.

He was rewarded when West showed out on the second round. He went back to dummy's spade and with dummy's ◊ 2 finessed East's ◊ J 7 with his ◊ Q 8.

If he still had the diamond ten in dummy, East would not cover.

DON'T COMPRESS YOUR TRICKS

```
                    ♠ A Q 2
                    ♡ A J 10 9
                    ◊ 8 6 4 3
                    ♣ A K
    ♠ J 9 7 6 4                    ♠ 10 8
    ♡ 8 3 2                        ♡ K 7 6
    ◊ A K J                        ◊ 7 2
    ♣ 8 5                          ♣ 10 9 7 6 3 2
                    ♠ K 5 3
                    ♡ Q 5 4
                    ◊ Q 10 9 5
                    ♣ Q J 4
```

Contract: 3 NT

Opening Lead: ♠ 6

Declarer started with what looked like lots of tricks. Three or four hearts, three spades, and three clubs. He won the opening lead with the spade king and took a heart finesse, leading the queen. East won and continued spades.

Declarer had now compressed his trick count to three spades, three hearts, and two clubs. He had no way back to his hand.

Down one. "What happened to your nine top tricks, partner? " asked North.

Question: What did happen? How would you have untangled this?

The other declarer took a simple line. She reasoned it might cost one trick, but it insured taking nine tricks. She won the opening lead in dummy and started the hearts immediately from the top.

Whoever had the heart king was welcome to it, but she had the spade king for a late entry to the queen of clubs.

Nine top tricks. Making 3 NT.

GETTING OUT OF YOUR OWN WAY

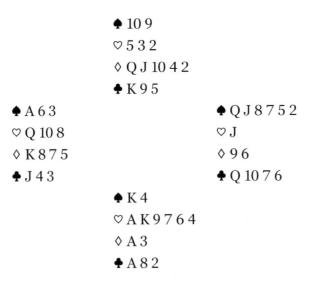

```
                    ♠ 10 9
                    ♡ 5 3 2
                    ◊ Q J 10 4 2
                    ♣ K 9 5
   ♠ A 6 3                          ♠ Q J 8 7 5 2
   ♡ Q 10 8                         ♡ J
   ◊ K 8 7 5                        ◊ 9 6
   ♣ J 4 3                          ♣ Q 10 7 6
                    ♠ K 4
                    ♡ A K 9 7 6 4
                    ◊ A 3
                    ♣ A 8 2
```

Contract: 4 ♡

Opening Lead: ◊ 5

Declarer played the queen from dummy which won the first trick. He cashed the A-K of trumps. Then declarer cashed the ace of diamonds and led a third trump. West won and exited a club.

Declarer ended losing two spades, one heart, and one club. Down one.

Question: Other than double dummy, what was a better line of play?

The other declarer made better use of his assets. After the same opening lead, he won the first diamond with the ace, unblocking the suit. After cashing his high trumps, he led his remaining low diamond.

All West could do was cash out to prevent an overtrick.

UNBLOCKING YOUR SECOND SUIT

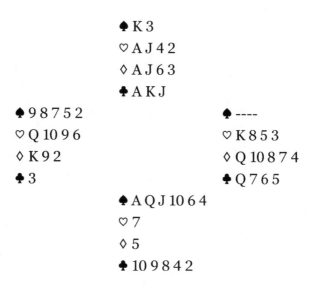

```
                        ♠ K 3
                        ♡ A J 4 2
                        ◇ A J 6 3
                        ♣ A K J
     ♠ 9 8 7 5 2                        ♠ ----
     ♡ Q 10 9 6                         ♡ K 8 5 3
     ◇ K 9 2                            ◇ Q 10 8 7 4
     ♣ 3                                ♣ Q 7 6 5
                        ♠ A Q J 10 6 4
                        ♡ 7
                        ◇ 5
                        ♣ 10 9 8 4 2
```

Contract: 6 ♠
Opening Lead: ♡ 10

South won the heart ace and cashed the trump king. When East showed out, declarer cashed the club ace, drew trumps and led a club to the king. When he led the club jack, East did well by ducking.

Declarer played the diamond ace and ruffed a diamond with his last trump. He lost a club and a heart. Down one.

Question: How would you have overcome the bad splits and good defense?

The other declarer, after cashing one round of clubs, drew trumps but discarded the blocking A-J of clubs. Now it was easy to lead clubs from his hand. He forced out the club queen while he still had trump control.

Making six spades, losing only one club.

UNBLOCKING YOUR SECOND SUIT

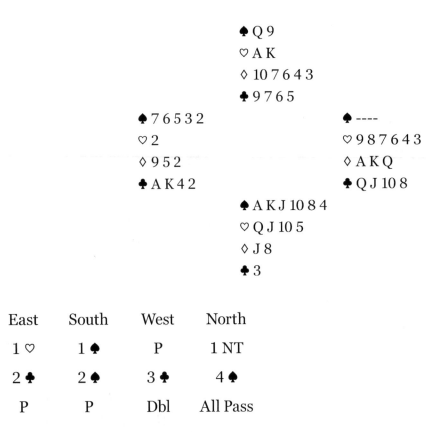

♠ Q 9
♡ A K
◊ 10 7 6 4 3
♣ 9 7 6 5

♠ 7 6 5 3 2
♡ 2
◊ 9 5 2
♣ A K 4 2

♠ ----
♡ 9 8 7 6 4 3
◊ A K Q
♣ Q J 10 8

♠ A K J 10 8 4
♡ Q J 10 5
◊ J 8
♣ 3

East	South	West	North
1 ♡	1 ♠	P	1 NT
2 ♣	2 ♠	3 ♣	4 ♠
P	P	Dbl	All Pass

Opening Lead: ♣ Ace

Declarer ruffed the second club. Four spades doubled looked easy until he played a trump to dummy's queen and East showed out. Declarer cashed the A-K of hearts, planning on then drawing the rest of the trumps.

Now with the top hearts out of the way, he could cash the rest of the hearts. But West ruffed the second heart and the defense took two diamond tricks.

Question: Was this a good plan or was there a better line of play?

There was no rush to cash the second heart. The other declarer cashed one high heart, and then drew all the trumps, unblocking dummy's last high heart.

He took six spade tricks and four heart tricks, one early and three later.

TRYING TO GET OUT OF YOUR OWN WAY

```
                    ♠ A K 2
                    ♡ A
                    ◊ 8 7 6 5
                    ♣ 9 8 7 6 5
      ♠ Q 9 3                      ♠ J 10 7 5
      ♡ Q 9 5                      ♡ J 10 7 6 2
      ◊ K J 3 2                    ◊ Q 10 9
      ♣ Q J 3                      ♣ 10
                    ♠ 8 6 4
                    ♡ K 8 4 3
                    ◊ A 4
                    ♣ A K 4 2
```

Contract: 3 NT
Opening Lead: ◊ 2

Declarer won the opening lead and cashed the A-K of clubs. He played a third club to West. West cashed his diamond winners and switched to the heart five.

In dummy, declarer took his club winners, but could not reach his king of hearts. He lost three diamonds, one club, and one spade. Down one.

Question: How can declarer untangle his nine winners? Cash the heart early?

The other declarer thought about cashing the heart ace early, then coming to his hand and cashing the heart king. But if he had to let the opponents in, he would go down even more.

Then he realized the best idea was to duck a club early. After the opponents cashed their diamonds, he could take his nine winners in peace. Early or later, it's all the same. Nine tricks are nine whenever you take them.

DECLARER BLOCKS HIMSELF

```
                    ♠ A K
                    ♡ Q J 10 9
                    ◊ 5 4 3 2
                    ♣ 8 6 4
        ♠ 10 9 7 6 4              ♠ 5 2
        ♡ K 4 2                   ♡ 7 6 5
        ◊ 10 6                    ◊ J 9 8 7
        ♣ J 9 2                   ♣ Q 10 5 3
                    ♠ Q J 8 3
                    ♡ A 8 3
                    ◊ A K Q
                    ♣ A K 7
```

Contract: 6 NT
Opening Lead: ♠ 10

Declarer counted lots of tricks. Being in dummy, there seemed to be no reason not to take a heart finesse. The queen of hearts won the trick. "Missed a grand, partner," said South. North just cringed.

Declarer led the heart jack and East played low. Declarer, probably thinking about thirteen tricks, finessed again. West won and played another spade.

Thirteen? Forget twelve. With the heart suit blocked, and no way back to the dummy and the good hearts, declarer finished down one.

Question: How would you have played 6 NT?

The other declarer received the same opening lead. He realized one finesse was probably safe, but he played a heart to his ace and led a small heart. If the defense ducked, he could continue hearts from the dummy.

Twelve tricks, the high spade was still in dummy to reach the good hearts if needed. Greed is not a good trait in a bridge player.

ULTIMATE DECLARER UNBLOCK

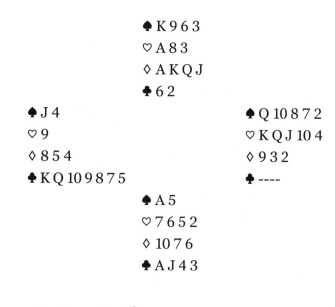

```
                    ♠ K 9 6 3
                    ♡ A 8 3
                    ◇ A K Q J
                    ♣ 6 2
      ♠ J 4                        ♠ Q 10 8 7 2
      ♡ 9                          ♡ K Q J 10 4
      ◇ 8 5 4                      ◇ 9 3 2
      ♣ K Q 10 9 8 7 5             ♣ ----
                    ♠ A 5
                    ♡ 7 6 5 2
                    ◇ 10 7 6
                    ♣ A J 4 3
```

West	North	East	South
3 ♣	Dbl	P	3 NT
	All Pass		

Opening Lead: ♣ King

Declarer ducked the first trick and West shifted to the heart nine. Declarer played low and East overtook to continue hearts. Declarer won the ace and played four rounds of diamonds.

After cashing the ace, then the king of spades, reducing West to all clubs, he played the club six to endplay West.

But West had carefully preserved the club five! East took the rest of the tricks.

Question: How did the other declarer make 3 NT?

At the other table, the play proceeded along the same lines. At trick ten, declarer led a club to endplay West who also had preserved the club five.

So what was the difference? At trick one, this declarer had unblocked the club six and so could lead the club two, not the six. West was endplayed. Another carefully preserved deuce.

15

PICK A PLAN: A, B, OR C

```
              ♠ A 7 4 3
              ♡ 8 5 2
              ◇ A K 6 4
              ♣ A K
♠ K Q J 2                    ♠ 10 8 6 5
♡ 7                          ♡ 9 6 4 3
◇ J 9 3                      ◇ Q 10 7 2
♣ J 6 5 4 2                  ♣ 3
              ♠ 9
              ♡ A K Q J 10
              ◇ 8 5
              ♣ Q 10 9 8 7
```

Contract: 6 ♡

Opening Lead: ♠ King

Declarer won the opening lead and started drawing trumps. West showed out on the second round. Declarer considered two lines of play before proceeding.

Plan A: Draw the rest of the trumps, cash the A-K of clubs, ruff a spade or diamond, then hope the club jack falls, or Plan B: Cash the A-K of clubs first and risk a club ruff. He chose one plan, but both were doomed. Down one.

Question: Was there a Plan C ?

Of course, that's why we are here. The other declarer cashed one high club. Then he finished drawing the trumps, discarding the remaining high club in dummy.

All that was left was to play clubs and drive out the club jack.

UNBLOCKING DRAWING TRUMPS

```
                          ♠ 7 3 2
                          ♡ A K
                          ◇ A 8 6 5 4
                          ♣ 6 5 4
        ♠ 10                              ♠ 9 8 6 5
        ♡ 9 8 7 6 4 3                     ♡ 2
        ◇ K Q J                           ◇ 7 2
        ♣ A K 8                           ♣ Q J 10 9 3 2
                          ♠ A K Q J 4
                          ♡ Q J 10 5
                          ◇ 10 9 3
                          ♣ 7
```

South	West	North	East
1 ♠	2 ♡	Dbl	P
2 ♠	P	4 ♠	All Pass

Opening Lead: ♣ Ace

West led the A-K of clubs. Declarer ruffed and played the A-K of trumps. West followed once, then discarded a heart.

Declarer played the A-K of hearts trying to get out of his own way, but East ruffed the second heart. South still had two diamond losers. Down one.

Question: Could you have managed to get out of your way?

At the other table, the declarer ruffed the second club. After playing the A-K of trumps, she cashed one round of hearts, then continued spades discarding dummy's remaining heart.

After drawing trumps, she played the Q-J-10 of hearts and had ten tricks.
Five spades, four hearts, and one diamond.

ANOTHER UNBLOCKING THE SECOND SUIT

```
                    ♠ 8 7 3 2
                    ♡ Q 9 8
                    ◇ 6 5 2
                    ♣ A K Q
        ♠ A K 10 5                 ♠ Q J 9 6
        ♡ 4                        ♡ 7 6 3 2
        ◇ A Q J 10 4               ◇ 9 8 3
        ♣ 10 9 6                   ♣ 4 2
                    ♠ 4
                    ♡ A K J 10 5
                    ◇ K 7
                    ♣ J 8 7 5 3
```

South	West	North	East
1 ♡	2 ◇	Dbl	P
3 ♣	P	3 ♡	P
4 ♡		All Pass	

Opening Lead: ♠ Ace

Declarer ruffed the second spade. When he cashed the A-J of trumps, West showed out. If he drew the rest of the trumps, how was he going to run the clubs?

He tried cashing the clubs in dummy. East ruffed and led a diamond. Down one.

Question: Was there a way to safely unblock the clubs?

Maybe. The other declarer cashed only two high clubs. Then he drew the remaining trumps and discarded dummy's last club. He took five hearts and five clubs for ten tricks.

18

MAKE AN OFFER

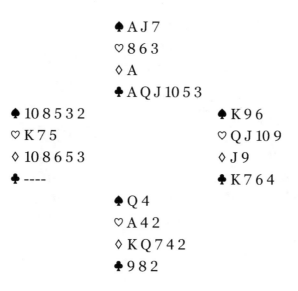

```
                        ♠ A J 7
                        ♡ 8 6 3
                        ◇ A
                        ♣ A Q J 10 5 3
        ♠ 10 8 5 3 2                        ♠ K 9 6
        ♡ K 7 5                             ♡ Q J 10 9
        ◇ 10 8 6 5 3                        ◇ J 9
        ♣ ----                              ♣ K 7 6 4
                        ♠ Q 4
                        ♡ A 4 2
                        ◇ K Q 7 4 2
                        ♣ 9 8 2
```

Contract: 3 NT

Opening Lead: ♠ 3

Declarer saw lots of tricks but playing low risked a dangerous heart shift. Declarer won the spade ace, unblocked the diamond ace, and played the A-Q of clubs. East played low. From this point, declarer was unable to untangle his tricks.

Question: Assuming East's good defense, was there a road home?

The other declarer tried to time his entries better. After unblocking the diamond ace, he offered the club queen first. When East ducked, declarer said "Would you like the jack?" When East ducked again, declarer, tired of that game, switched back to spades.

Now he had three clubs, two spades, one heart, and three diamonds. Nine tricks.

DISCARDING TO UNBLOCK

```
              ♠ A 6 3 2
              ♡ J 2
              ◇ K 5 4 3 2
              ♣ J 4
♠ K Q 10 8 7 4              ♠ 5
♡ 8 5 4                    ♡ Q 10 9 7 3
◇ 9                        ◇ J 10 6
♣ Q 8 7                    ♣ K 10 6 5
              ♠ J 9
              ♡ A K 6
              ◇ A Q 8 7
              ♣ A 9 3 2
```

Contract: 3 NT

Opening Lead: ♠ King

Declarer won the opening lead and quickly claimed nine tricks. But the defenders were awake and the claim was rejected. Declarer finally saw the problem, but there was no solution.

He had no way back to the last diamond. Down one.

Question: How can declarer unblock the diamonds?

The other declarer ducked the first spade. West shifted to a club. Declarer won the third club and played the spade jack. West won, but now declarer could discard a diamond from his hand on the spade ace.

He took five diamonds, one spade, two hearts, and one club.

UNBLOCKING WINNERS

Eddie Kantar showed a nice example of getting out of your way in the ACBL "Bulletin" January, 2021. See how you would do with this: No peeking below.

♠ A K
♥ A 3 2
♦ Q J 10 9 7 6 4 3
♣ ----

♠ Q J 10 9 8
♥ K Q J 10 6
♦ ----
♣ A 7 4

Eddie writes, "Desperate for a huge swing ...., you wind up in 7 ♥ against silent opponents. The opening lead is the ♣ King." Over to you.

Solution: "Ruff the club in dummy, ruff a diamond low, ruff a club with the ♥ A, draw trumps and discard the ♠ A K on winning hearts. You remain with all winning spades and the ♣ A. The traps are (a) not to play the ♠ A K prematurely because someone may have a singleton spade, and (b) to ruff the diamond low. You need four high hearts in your hand to draw trumps, as they may be 4-1." The complete hand:

♠ A K
♥ A 3 2
♦ Q J 10 9 7
6 4 3
♣ ----

♠ 6 5 4 3 2   ♠ 7
♥ 7   ♥ 9 8 5 4
♦ K 8 2   ♦ A 5
♣ K Q 10 6   ♣ J 9 8 5 3 2

♠ Q J 10 9 8
♥ K Q J 10 6
♦ ----
♣ A 7 4   Thanks, Eddie. You are the best!

MAINTAINING CONTROL

```
                    ♠ J 7 6
                    ♡ K 3 2
                    ◇ A J 3 2
                    ♣ A K Q
   ♠ A K Q 10 4                      ♠ 8 5 3
   ♡ 8 6                             ♡ 10 9 7 5
   ◇ K 8 5                           ◇ Q 10 9 4
   ♣ 8 6 2                           ♣ 9 7
                    ♠ 9 2
                    ♡ A Q J 4
                    ◇ 7 6
                    ♣ J 10 5 4 3
```

Contract: 4 ♡

Opening Lead: ♠ Ace

West led the A-K-Q of spades. Declarer ruffed the third spade. When East turned up with four trumps, declarer lost control trying to cash and unblock the clubs.

Question: 4/3 fits are difficult and a blocked side suit. But can you handle this?

At the other table, the declarer's first good play was not ruffing the third heart. He discarded a diamond, a trick he would lose anyhow. He won the diamond continuation and cashed the A-K of trumps. Then he cashed the A-K of clubs, both defenders followed. OK, almost there.

He played two more rounds of trumps and on the second round, discarded the blocking club queen. The way was clear to cash three more club tricks in his hand.
He lost only three spade tricks. Making four hearts.

WHICH SUIT TO SET UP ?

                    ♠ Q J 10 9 5
                    ♡ K 3 2
                    ◊ A K 4
                    ♣ 6 2
    ♠ K 3 2   ♠ 8 7 6 4
    ♡ 4   ♡ J 10 6
    ◊ Q J 10 8 2   ◊ 7 6 5 3
    ♣ K 10 8 4   ♣ J 3
                    ♠ A
                    ♡ A Q 9 8 7 5
                    ◊ 9
                    ♣ A Q 9 7 5

Contract: 6 ♡

Opening Lead: ◊ Queen

Declarer won the opening lead. He decided to try to set up the clubs and led a club to his queen. West won the king and returned another diamond. Declarer discarded a club and played a club to his ace. He ruffed a club with the trump king and played a heart to his ace.

When he cashed the heart queen, East's heart jack was the setting trick.

Question: Was there a better line of play?

Much better, almost 100%. The other declarer went for the spade suit. Only one dummy entry remained, and the suit was blocked. Easily remedied, declarer cashed the diamond king, discarding the spade ace from his hand. Now he played the spade queen.

West won the king, the only trick for the defenders. Declarer drew trumps ending in the dummy and the spades took care of business.

Note if declarer's spade was the king, he would need to make the same unblocking play. If he led a spade to the king, West could defeat the slam by ducking the ace.

UNBLOCKING BY A BIG DISCARD

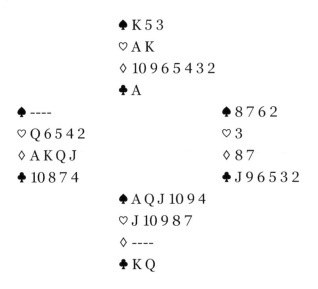

♠ K 5 3
♡ A K
♢ 10 9 6 5 4 3 2
♣ A

♠ ----
♡ Q 6 5 4 2
♢ A K Q J
♣ 10 8 7 4

♠ 8 7 6 2
♡ 3
♢ 8 7
♣ J 9 6 5 3 2

♠ A Q J 10 9 4
♡ J 10 9 8 7
♢ ----
♣ K Q

Contract: 6 ♠

Opening Lead: ♢ Ace

Declarer ruffed the opening lead and played the ace of trumps. When West showed out, he cashed the A-K of hearts. East ruffed the second heart and returned a trump. South won and led the heart jack. West played low and declarer had no good option.

If he did not ruff, East would. If he ruffed high, he had a heart loser at the end. Down one.

Question: How would you have untangled all these assets?

The other declarer had seen this problem before. But it was not a problem. He ruffed the opening lead and drew trumps. On the fourth round of trumps, he discarded the club ace, unblocking the suit.

After knocking out the heart queen, he still had a trump. His hand was high. He lost one heart, making six spades.

UNBLOCKING HIGH CARDS TO GET OUT OF YOUR WAY

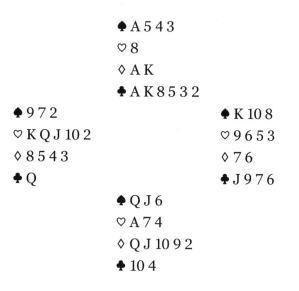

♠ A 5 4 3
♡ 8
◇ A K
♣ A K 8 5 3 2

♠ 9 7 2
♡ K Q J 10 2
◇ 8 5 4 3
♣ Q

♠ K 10 8
♡ 9 6 5 3
◇ 7 6
♣ J 9 7 6

♠ Q J 6
♡ A 7 4
◇ Q J 10 9 2
♣ 10 4

Contract: 3 NT
Opening Lead: ♡ King

Declarer ducked two rounds of hearts, discarding low spades from dummy. He won the third heart and cashed the A-K of diamonds. He led a low spade from dummy, but East won and the defense cashed two more heart tricks. Down one.

Question: All those assets, could you have put them to better use?

The other declarer made 3 NT by unblocking some of those fine assets. At trick two he ducked the heart but discarded a high diamond.

If West continued hearts, he would discard the other diamond honor, winning the heart in hand. With the diamonds unblocked, he would have nine tricks.

If West realized what was happening and switched after trick two to a club, declarer would win, unblock the remaining high diamond, and lead a low spade assuring an entry to his hand.

GETTING OUT OF MY OWN WAY

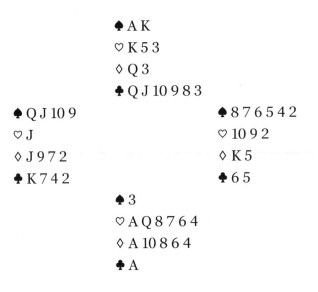

♠ A K
♡ K 5 3
◊ Q 3
♣ Q J 10 9 8 3

♠ Q J 10 9
♡ J
◊ J 9 7 2
♣ K 7 4 2

♠ 8 7 6 5 4 2
♡ 10 9 2
◊ K 5
♣ 6 5

♠ 3
♡ A Q 8 7 6 4
◊ A 10 8 6 4
♣ A

Contract: 6 ♡

Opening Lead: ♠ Queen

Declarer won the opening lead and played a club to his ace. He led a low diamond to the queen and king. East's trump return was won in dummy. Declarer played the diamond ace and ruffed a diamond, but East overruffed and returned his last trump.

Down two. North sat in stunned silence. "What?" asked South.

Question: What do you think North wanted to say? How would you have played?

Another example of too many assets. The other declarer set up the club suit instead. The club ace is in the way? No problem, draw trumps and throw the club ace away under the A-K of spades.

West can try to hold on to his club king, and East may try to ruff in, but declarer can simply overruff. He might end up with an overtrick.

UNBLOCKING IN TIME

```
                    ♠ 10 5 4 2
                    ♡ K Q
                    ◇ A 9 6 5
                    ♣ A Q J
      ♠ 7 6                           ♠ K Q J 9
      ♡ J 10 9 8 3                    ♡ 7 6 4
      ◇ K 10 4 2                      ◇ J 8 7
      ♣ 7 6                           ♣ K 5 3
                    ♠ A 8 3
                    ♡ A 5 2
                    ◇ Q 3
                    ♣ 10 9 8 4 2
```

Contract: 3 NT
Opening Lead: ♡ Jack

Declarer won the heart king in dummy. Needing only four club tricks, he played clubs from the top to preserve his spade ace. East won the second club and returned the king of spades. Everything was blocked.

Declarer ducked and won the spade continuation. He crossed to the jack of clubs and belatedly cashed heart queen. When he led a diamond to his queen, West won and the contract was doomed.

Question: How could declarer have better timed his play?

The other declarer unblocked the remaining high heart honor in dummy first. Then he unblocked the club jack under the heart ace, and took his nine tricks.

Four clubs, one diamond, three hearts, and one spade.

DECLARER BLOCKS OUT OTHER OPTIONS

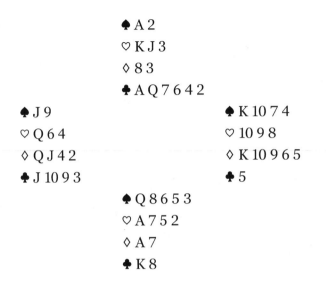

                    ♠ A 2
                    ♡ K J 3
                    ◊ 8 3
                    ♣ A Q 7 6 4 2

    ♠ J 9   ♠ K 10 7 4
    ♡ Q 6 4   ♡ 10 9 8
    ◊ Q J 4 2   ◊ K 10 9 6 5
    ♣ J 10 9 3   ♣ 5

                    ♠ Q 8 6 5 3
                    ♡ A 7 5 2
                    ◊ A 7
                    ♣ K 8

Contract: 3 NT

Opening Lead: ◊ 2

West made the most damaging opening lead. Declarer won and needed the next eight tricks. He cashed the club king and led a club to the ace. When East showed out, the contract was unmakeable. Other options such as the heart suit were no longer available.

"Partner, can't you ask yourself what might go wrong before, not after it happens?" asked North, writing – 100.

Question: Could you have not blocked yourself into a no-win situation?

The other declarer, to keep her options open and not get blocked out, did things the other way. She cashed the ace, then the king of clubs ending in her hand. If clubs were 3-2, she had an entry to the dummy and nine tricks.

If not, the other option of 3-3 hearts with the queen onside was still available. "Good thinking ahead, partner," said North, writing + 600.

ENTRY
PROBLEMS

UNBLOCKING TO CREATE AN ENTRY

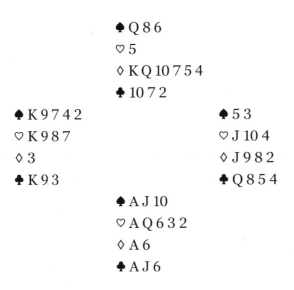

```
                    ♠ Q 8 6
                    ♡ 5
                    ◊ K Q 10 7 5 4
                    ♣ 10 7 2
    ♠ K 9 7 4 2                        ♠ 5 3
    ♡ K 9 8 7                          ♡ J 10 4
    ◊ 3                                ◊ J 9 8 2
    ♣ K 9 3                            ♣ Q 8 5 4
                    ♠ A J 10
                    ♡ A Q 6 3 2
                    ◊ A 6
                    ♣ A J 6
```

Contract: 3 NT

Opening Lead: ♠ 4

Declarer won the first trick in hand with the ten of spades. He played the diamond ace and led his small diamond. When West showed out, play slowed. He won the K-Q of diamonds, but he had no way back to dummy even if he set up the rest of the diamonds.

There were not nine tricks. "Partner," moaned North, "You had nine sure tricks. What happened?"

Question: Do you see what happened?

As Mike Lawrence says, having and taking are not the same. The contract was only at risk if one defender had ◊ J-x-x-x. And that could be overcome as long as declarer had a dummy entry.

The other declarer won trick one with the spade ace, almost for sure guaranteeing the spade queen as a later entry. After conceding a diamond, he had nine tricks. Two spades, one heart, five diamonds and one club.

BASIC UNBLOCKING TO CREATE AN ENTRY

```
                      ♠ K 9 3
                      ♡ 4 2
                      ◇ K Q J 10 7 6
                      ♣ 8 5
    ♠ Q 10 7 6 4                       ♠ 8 5 2
    ♡ A 6 3                            ♡ K 10 9
    ◇ 9                                ◇ A 8 3
    ♣ J 10 7 3                         ♣ Q 9 6 2
                      ♠ A J
                      ♡ Q J 8 7 5
                      ◇ 5 4 2
                      ♣ A K 4
```

Contract: 3 NT
Opening Lead: ♠ 6

Declarer won the opening lead with his jack and led a diamond. East won the third round of diamonds and returned a spade. You could hear North's teeth.

Question: How should declarer have played?

Slower, and with more thought. No free gifts. The other declarer won the first trick with the spade ace, no free gifts, thank you. He had an entry later to the good diamonds.

I was almost embarrassed to put this easy hand in my book, but I played with someone who won the jack so....... Those were my teeth you heard gnashing.

UNBLOCKING ENTRY PROBLEMS

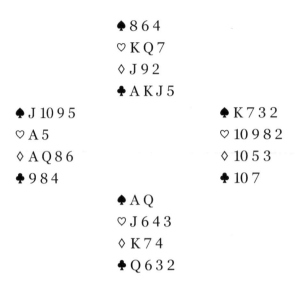

```
                    ♠ 8 6 4
                    ♡ K Q 7
                    ◊ J 9 2
                    ♣ A K J 5
    ♠ J 10 9 5                    ♠ K 7 3 2
    ♡ A 5                         ♡ 10 9 8 2
    ◊ A Q 8 6                     ◊ 10 5 3
    ♣ 9 8 4                       ♣ 10 7
                    ♠ A Q
                    ♡ J 6 4 3
                    ◊ K 7 4
                    ♣ Q 6 3 2
```

Contract: 3 NT
Opening Lead: ♠ Jack

Declarer captured East's king with the ace at trick one. He led a heart to the king which held. He played a club to his queen and led another heart, West winning the ace. West played another spade.

Declarer had two good hearts, but no way to untangle his tricks. He could cash the heart in dummy, but he had no way back to his hand. Down one.

Question: How did the declarer at the other table make 3 NT?

The other declarer looked ahead and foresaw the problem. Play started the same way, declarer playing a heart at trick two. But then he cashed the A-K of clubs. When both defenders followed, he came to his hand by playing the club jack to the queen.

By unblocking the clubs, he had a second entry to his hand, the club five to the six, to be able to later untangle the good hearts. He scored four clubs, two spades, and three hearts. Nine tricks.

UNBLOCKING IN TRUMPS TO CREATE ENTRIES

♠ Q J 10 7
♡ K 4 3
♢ 7 5 4 3
♣ J 7

♠ 5
♡ Q J 10 7 5
♢ 9 2
♣ 10 8 5 3 2

♠ K 4 3
♡ A 9 2
♢ K 10 6
♣ K 9 6 4

♠ A 9 8 6 2
♡ 8 6
♢ A Q J 8
♣ A Q

East	South	West	North
1 ♣	1 ♠	P	2 ♠
P	4 ♠	All Pass	

Opening Lead: ♡ Queen

The defense started with two rounds of hearts, then declarer ruffed the third heart. He had finesse positions in three suits which rated to win, but limited entries. He cashed the ace of trumps, no king. He led a spade to East's king, but East had a third spade to exit.

Declarer took a successful minor suit finesse, then went back to dummy with a trump and took another successful minor suit finesse. He cashed the diamond ace, no king. Lacking one more entry, down one.

Question: Was there another entry in the house?

The other declarer faced the same problem. But at trick three, he ruffed the third heart with the spade ace! Now when he gave East the trump king, he had an extra entry in spades to finesse twice in diamonds and once in clubs.
Making four spades.

33

UNBLOCKING TO CREATE A NEEDED ENTRY

```
                    ♠ K Q 9 6
                    ♡ A J 10 7
                    ◇ A K 6
                    ♣ J 3
        ♠ A 4                      ♠ 8 5
        ♡ K 4 3 2                  ♡ Q 6
        ◇ Q 10 9                   ◇ 7 4 3 2
        ♣ A K Q 5                  ♣ 10 9 8 4 2
                    ♠ J 10 7 3 2
                    ♡ 9 8 5
                    ◇ J 8 5
                    ♣ 7 6
```

West	North	East	South
1 ♣	Dbl	P	1 ♠
Dbl	3 ♠	All Pass	

Opening Lead: ♣ Ace

West cashed the A-K of clubs and switched to the ace of spades, followed by a low spade. Declarer won the second spade in his hand and took a heart finesse. East won and returned a diamond. Declarer played low, nine, king.

Declarer cashed the diamond ace hoping to drop the queen. Down one.

Question: Good effort. Could you have done better?

The other declarer saw an extra opportunity. West opened and doubled, but split heart honors were possible. Declarer needed entries to take two heart finesses.

Play started the same, but at trick three, when West played the spade ace, this declarer unblocked the spade king from dummy. Now he had two trump entries to his hand. He took two heart finesses. Making three spades. Whew, not much, pair of jacks, but just enough.

SAVING YOUR ENTRY FOR AFTER UNBLOCKING

```
                        ♠ A Q 5 2
                        ♡ A J 4
                        ◊ 5 4
                        ♣ J 10 9 8
        ♠ K 4                            ♠ J 9 8 7 6
        ♡ 10 8 7 5                       ♡ Q 9 3
        ◊ A Q J 9 7 3                    ◊ 10 8 2
        ♣ 3                              ♣ Q 5
                        ♠ 10 3
                        ♡ K 6 2
                        ◊ K 6
                        ♣ A K 7 6 4 2
```

South	West	North	East
1 ♣	1 ◊	1 ♠	P
2 ♣	P	2◊	P
2 NT	P	3 NT	All Pass

Opening Lead: ♡ 5

Declarer, perhaps too quickly, played the jack, thinking West had probably led from ♡ Q 10 x x. East played the queen and declarer had to win to avoid a diamond switch. He cashed the A-K of clubs and another club.

Then finally a light went off as he realized he was going to take four, not six club tricks. So much for 3 NT. And he could not come back now to take a spade finesse.

Question: How should declarer have played for nine sure tricks?

Slower, at trick one. Yes, the clubs are blocked, but as long as declarer keeps an entry to his hand, the heart king, for later, (whenever that may be), he has nine tricks. But having them and taking them are two different things.

Win the heart ace at trick one. Take two clubs from his hand, then two from the dummy, then back for two more. One spade, two hearts, and six clubs.

UNBLOCKING TO CREATE AN ENTRY

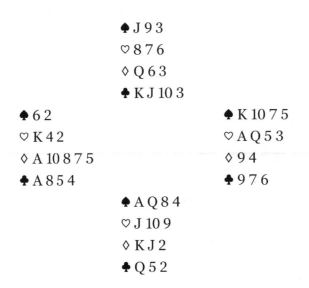

```
                        ♠ J 9 3
                        ♡ 8 7 6
                        ◊ Q 6 3
                        ♣ K J 10 3
        ♠ 6 2                         ♠ K 10 7 5
        ♡ K 4 2                       ♡ A Q 5 3
        ◊ A 10 8 7 5                  ◊ 9 4
        ♣ A 8 5 4                     ♣ 9 7 6
                        ♠ A Q 8 4
                        ♡ J 10 9
                        ◊ K J 2
                        ♣ Q 5 2
```

Contract: 1 NT

Opening Lead: ◊ 7

On the first trick East played the nine, declarer won the jack. He started the clubs. West won the third club and switched to a heart. East won the ace and reverted to diamonds.

Declarer wanted to reach dummy to cash the good club and take a spade finesse. But he had no entry. If he played the diamond king, West would duck. If he played low, West would win and return a diamond, blocking the suit. Sad.

Question: Such a headache, such an easy solution. Do you see it?

Mike Lawrence says some of the most innocent plays in bridge can come back to haunt you in the strangest of ways.

The other declarer won trick one with the king, not the jack. He could not be prevented from reaching dummy's diamond queen.

He took at least two spades, two diamonds, and three clubs.

UNBLOCKING TO PROVIDE AN ENTRY

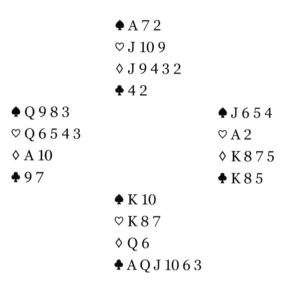

♠ A 7 2
♥ J 10 9
♦ J 9 4 3 2
♣ 4 2

♠ Q 9 8 3
♥ Q 6 5 4 3
♦ A 10
♣ 9 7

♠ J 6 5 4
♥ A 2
♦ K 8 7 5
♣ K 8 5

♠ K 10
♥ K 8 7
♦ Q 6
♣ A Q J 10 6 3

Contract: 3 NT (Overbid a bit?)

Opening Lead: ♥ 4

East won the opening lead and returned the suit. Declarer won, went to dummy with a spade and took a successful club finesse. He cashed the club ace. When the king did not fall, there was no road to 3 NT.

Question: How did the other declarer find a road to 3 NT?

She made a good trade. Give one, get five, not bad? At trick one, she unblocked the heart king under the ace. That cost an early heart trick, but now with two entries to dummy, she was able to take two club finesses.

She took six club tricks. Pretty good trade.

SAME UNBLOCKING, JUST MORE ENTRIES

                        ♠ K 6 3
                        ♡ J 10 9
                        ◊ A J 5 2
                        ♣ 8 6 4

        ♠ Q 10 9   ♠ 8 7 5 2
        ♡ Q 7 6 5 2   ♡ A 4
        ◊ 10 6 3   ◊ K Q 9
        ♣ 7 2   ♣ K 9 5 3

                        ♠ A J 4
                        ♡ K 8 3
                        ◊ 8 7 4
                        ♣ A Q J 10

Contract: 3 NT
Opening Lead: ♡ 5

East won the opening lead and returned the suit. Declarer, having just played the previous hand, thought, "Well, at least this time I have enough entries, I don't have to waste my heart king under the ace." She won the heart king in hand at trick two.

She went to dummy with a spade and took a successful club finesse. She went back to dummy with a diamond and repeated the club finesse. When she cashed the club ace, the king did not drop. Whoops, no 3 NT.

Question: What can we learn from this?

You can 'never' have too many entries. The other declarer unblocked the heart king at trick one, just in case he needed one more club finesse. Making 3 NT.

BLOCKED SUITS AND ENTRY PROBLEMS

```
                        ♠ K J 9 4
                        ♡ Q 5 2
                        ◊ A 6 2
                        ♣ 8 5 3
        ♠ 10 7 6 5                      ♠ 8 3
        ♡ 7                             ♡ K 8 6 4
        ◊ K Q 10 7                      ◊ J 9 5
        ♣ A K J 2                       ♣ 10 9 6 4
                        ♠ A Q 2
                        ♡ A J 10 9 3
                        ◊ 8 4 3
                        ♣ Q 7
```

South	West	North	East
1 ♡	Dbl	Rdbl	P
P	2 ♣	2 ♡	P
4 ♡		All Pass	

Opening Lead: ♣ Ace

West switched to the diamond king at trick two. Declarer won and led the trump queen and a trump to his jack. Then he led the two of spades to dummy's jack and repeated the trump finesse.

But with the spade suit now blocked, West saved his spades and declarer ended losing two clubs and two diamonds. Down one.

Question: Was there a way to untangle his assets and take ten tricks?

The other declarer at trick five led the queen of spades to dummy's king, not the deuce. After drawing trumps, he cashed the spade ace and led the spade deuce to dummy's ♠ J-9, and played the nine, playing West for four spades to the ten based on the bidding. He discarded a loser on the long spade.

Making four hearts.

39

UNBLOCKING TO CREATE AN ENTRY
TO DECLARER'S HAND

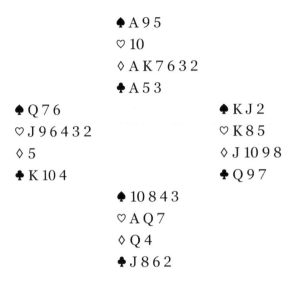

♠ A 9 5
♡ 10
♢ A K 7 6 3 2
♣ A 5 3

♠ Q 7 6   ♠ K J 2
♡ J 9 6 4 3 2   ♡ K 8 5
♢ 5   ♢ J 10 9 8
♣ K 10 4   ♣ Q 9 7

♠ 10 8 4 3
♡ A Q 7
♢ Q 4
♣ J 8 6 2

Contract: 3 NT
Opening Lead: ♡ 4

East played the king at trick one and declarer won the ace. Seeing ten tricks, but not planning ahead, declarer cashed the diamond queen and led a diamond. West showed out.

OK, he thought, only nine tricks. He cashed the A-K of diamonds and played a fourth diamond. But East returned a club. Now he was down to eight tricks.

The heart queen is still sitting in declarer's hand as you read this sad tale.

Question: How did the other declarer survive? Sloppy defense?

No, he unblocked his tricks by playing a low diamond from both hands at trick two. This assured the contract against a 4-1 split, and preserved an entry to the queen of hearts.

Bridge is an easy game, what was the problem?

UNBLOCKING TO CREATE AN ENTRY TO THE DUMMY

Frank Stewart always has wonderful hands in his daily newspaper columns. Here is one from a few years ago in which Frank said, "Requires a degree of perfection that not many declarers could produce."

```
                        ♠ A Q J
                        ♡ J 10 3
                        ◊ J 10 7 6 4
                        ♣ 6 3
        ♠ 9                          ♠ K 10 8 5
        ♡ K 9 7 4 2                  ♡ 8 6 5
        ◊ Q 3 2                      ◊ 9 8 5
        ♣ Q 8 5 2                    ♣ J 7 4
                        ♠ 7 6 4 3 2
                        ♡ A Q
                        ◊ A K
                        ♣ A K 10 9
```

Contract: 3 NT
Opening Lead: ♡ 4

Declarer won the heart queen and led a spade to the queen. East won and returned a heart. Declarer cashed the A-K of diamonds, no queen. He led a second spade. South could only take eight tricks before the defense ran the hearts.

Question: How did Frank suggest declarer play?

After declarer wins the first heart and cashes the A-K of diamonds, play a spade to the ace. Now lead the diamond jack, discarding the heart ace! At some point, the defense must allow declarer to reach dummy.

He has four diamonds, two hearts, one spade, and two clubs. That's nine big ones! Thanks, Frank.

ENTRIES AND SPOT CARDS MEAN A LOT

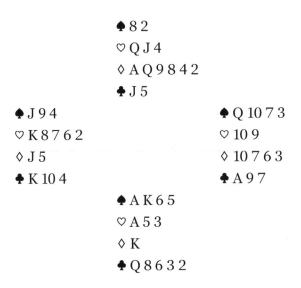

<pre>
                    ♠ 8 2
                    ♡ Q J 4
                    ◊ A Q 9 8 4 2
                    ♣ J 5
   ♠ J 9 4   ♠ Q 10 7 3
   ♡ K 8 7 6 2   ♡ 10 9
   ◊ J 5   ◊ 10 7 6 3
   ♣ K 10 4   ♣ A 9 7
                    ♠ A K 6 5
                    ♡ A 5 3
                    ◊ K
                    ♣ Q 8 6 3 2
</pre>

Contract: 3 NT
Opening Lead: ♡ 6

Declarer made a good play by winning the first trick with the ace, not an honor from dummy. He unblocked the diamond king, then lead a low heart. West played low and declarer won the queen.

He cashed the A-Q of diamonds, but the diamonds divided 4-2 and the contract was doomed.

Question: Could you have made use of some hidden assets to bring this home?

The other declarer wasn't blinded by the high cards. Spot cards are important. Realizing the odds were against a 3-3 split, she also won the heart lead with the ace. But she played the diamond king to the ace, cashed the diamond queen and led the diamond nine. With a sure entry in hearts, the diamonds were now high.

She had two spades, two hearts, and five diamonds.

FORCING AN ENTRY FOR REPEATED FINESSES

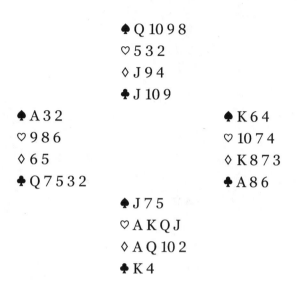

♠ Q 10 9 8
♥ 5 3 2
♦ J 9 4
♣ J 10 9

♠ A 3 2
♥ 9 8 6
♦ 6 5
♣ Q 7 5 3 2

♠ K 6 4
♥ 10 7 4
♦ K 8 7 3
♣ A 8 6

♠ J 7 5
♥ A K Q J
♦ A Q 10 2
♣ K 4

Contract: 3 NT

Opening Lead: ♣ 3

Declarer started well, unblocking the club king under East's ace, to assure a dummy entry. East returned the club eight, West won and continued the suit. Declarer needed four diamond tricks, so he led the diamond jack and took a winning finesse. He continued with the diamond nine, winning in hand.

But when he played the ace, the king did not fall. North said, "Partner, after making the hard play, how could you miss the easy play?" Down one.

Question: What was North referring to?

The other declarer also made the good unblocking play at trick one, the hard part of this hand. The rest was easy; stay in the dummy as long as possible for repeated diamond finesses. He started with the diamond nine, underplaying the two. Then the jack, underplaying the ten.

And finally one more for the road. Low to the A-Q. Nine tricks. Making 3 NT.

UNBLOCKING TO PROVIDE AN EXTRA ENTRY

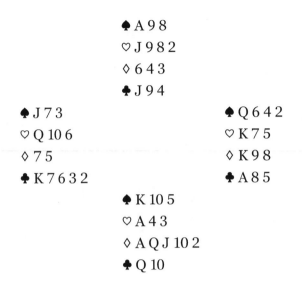

♠ A 9 8
♡ J 9 8 2
♢ 6 4 3
♣ J 9 4

♠ J 7 3　　　　　　　　　♠ Q 6 4 2
♡ Q 10 6　　　　　　　　♡ K 7 5
♢ 7 5　　　　　　　　　　♢ K 9 8
♣ K 7 6 3 2　　　　　　　♣ A 8 5

♠ K 10 5
♡ A 4 3
♢ A Q J 10 2
♣ Q 10

Contract:　3 NT

Opening Lead:　♣ 3

East won the ace and returned the eight, declarer playing the ten, then the queen. West ducked, hoping East had an entry and another club. Declarer played a spade to dummy and took a successful diamond finesse.

With no second entry, he cashed the diamond ace. When the king did not fall, the contract was doomed.

Question: How did declarer make 3 NT in the other room?

At trick one, declarer unblocked the club queen under the ace. When the defense allowed declarer to win trick two, he was in the dummy. He could take two diamond finesses.

If West had won trick two, declarer could withstand a switch to another suit since the defender's clubs had not yet been established.

UNBLOCKING AN ACE TO CREATE AN ENTRY

```
                    ♠ 6 4 3
                    ♡ 10 4
                    ◊ K J 10 9 5
                    ♣ Q 7 5
        ♠ J 7 5                     ♠ Q 9 8 2
        ♡ K 6 3                     ♡ J 9 8 5
        ◊ 8 4                       ◊ A 7 2
        ♣ K J 8 6 2                 ♣ 9 3
                    ♠ A K 10
                    ♡ A Q 7 2
                    ◊ Q 6 3
                    ♣ A 10 4
```

Contract: 3 NT

Opening Lead: ♣ 6

At trick one East played the nine, declarer won the ten. He started the diamonds. West played the eight and East ducked two rounds. East won the third round and played a club. Declarer had no way to reach the dummy.

South finished down two.

Question: Overbid or what? Was there a way home?

The other declarer saw a better road. After East played the nine, using the Rule of Eleven, he reasoned West held the club king. He won the first trick with the ace, unblocking the suit. The queen of clubs was a sure entry to dummy.

He scored two clubs, four diamonds, and three major suit tricks.

UNBLOCKING TO CREATE AN ENTRY

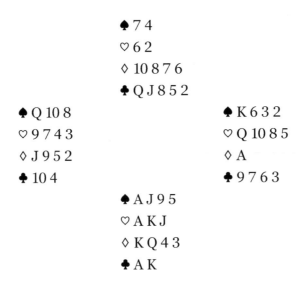

♠ 7 4
♡ 6 2
◊ 10 8 7 6
♣ Q J 8 5 2

♠ Q 10 8
♡ 9 7 4 3
◊ J 9 5 2
♣ 10 4

♠ K 6 3 2
♡ Q 10 8 5
◊ A
♣ 9 7 6 3

♠ A J 9 5
♡ A K J
◊ K Q 4 3
♣ A K

Contract: 3 NT
Opening Lead: ◊ 2

East won the opening lead and returned a heart. Declarer played the jack, winning. He cashed his minor suit winners, but when the diamond jack did not fall (no surprise), he finished with eight tricks. Down one.

Question: By now I'm sure you see the correct play, don't you?

The other declarer unblocked a high diamond honor under the ace at trick one. East's best return was a spade. South would play the nine, West the ten and continue with the queen.

Declarer would win, cash the A-K of clubs, then the diamond king and a low diamond. The defenders could score two diamonds and two spades.
Declarer had saved a low diamond to reach dummy's clubs. Nine tricks.

BASIC UNBLOCKING TO ASSURE A DUMMY ENTRY

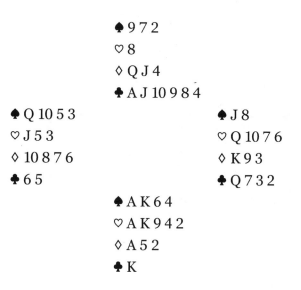

                    ♠ 9 7 2
                    ♡ 8
                    ◇ Q J 4
                    ♣ A J 10 9 8 4
    ♠ Q 10 5 3   ♠ J 8
    ♡ J 5 3   ♡ Q 10 7 6
    ◇ 10 8 7 6   ◇ K 9 3
    ♣ 6 5   ♣ Q 7 3 2
                    ♠ A K 6 4
                    ♡ A K 9 4 2
                    ◇ A 5 2
                    ♣ K

Contract: 3 NT

Opening Lead: ◇ 6

Declarer played the queen from dummy, East played low. Declarer started the clubs from the top to drive out the queen. East won and returned a heart.

Declarer had no way back to the dummy and finished down one.

Question: What happened to the dummy entry?

The other declarer simply won the opening lead with the ace. He then led the club king, overtaking with the ace. When the clubs were established, he had two small diamonds and could not be prevented from reaching dummy.

Lots of tricks.

CAREFUL UNBLOCKING FOR ENTRY PRESERVATION

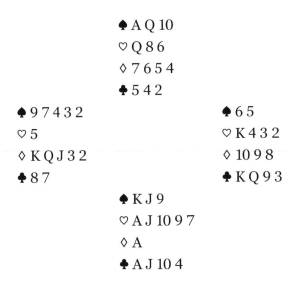

♠ A Q 10
♡ Q 8 6
◊ 7 6 5 4
♣ 5 4 2

♠ 9 7 4 3 2
♡ 5
◊ K Q J 3 2
♣ 8 7

♠ 6 5
♡ K 4 3 2
◊ 10 9 8
♣ K Q 9 3

♠ K J 9
♡ A J 10 9 7
◊ A
♣ A J 10 4

Contract: 6 ♡

Opening Lead: ◊ King

Declarer won the opening lead and played a spade to dummy's queen. He led the heart queen; low, low, low. He led another heart, winning in hand. He played the spade nine to the ten to repeat the heart finesse.

OK, club time. He had one more entry in spades and led a club; queen, ace. He had no more entries to dummy to lead another club. He played the club jack to East's queen, but he still had another losing club.

Question: Was there any way to reach dummy to lead clubs again?

The other declarer started the same, but when he led the heart queen, he unblocked the nine from his hand to stay in the dummy. Next came the heart eight, playing the seven from hand. Finally, one more heart finesse.

He still had two spade entries to lead clubs thru East. He made six hearts, losing only one club trick.

KEEPING YOURSELF BLOCKED TO PROVIDE AN ENTRY

          ♠ A 5 4 3
          ♡ 10 7 6 4
          ◊ K Q
          ♣ 10 4 3

♠ K 10 8 2   ♠ Q 9 6
♡ Q J 8   ♡ K 9 3 2
◊ J 6 3   ◊ 8 7 4
♣ J 8 6   ♣ A 9 7

          ♠ J 7
          ♡ A 5
          ◊ A 10 9 5 2
          ♣ K Q 5 2

Contract: 3 NT
Opening Lead: ♠ 2

Declarer ducked the opening lead. East won the queen and returned a spade. Declarer won the ace, cashed the K-Q of diamonds to unblock the suit, and led a club. East played low and declarer won the king.

He cashed the diamond ace. Good news: diamonds were 3-3. Bad news: declarer could only take eight tricks. He led a low club, hoping the ace was now singleton. Down one.

Question: Pushy contract sure, but was there a road home?

At the other table, play started the same, but declarer only unblocked one diamond honor. He left the suit blocked and led a club at trick four. East played low. When declarer won the club king, he led to the remaining diamond honor in dummy and led another club.

It didn't matter whether East won or ducked. With clubs also 3-3, declarer had ten tricks. Five diamonds, three clubs, and two major suit aces.

UNBLOCKING TO CREATE A STEPPING STONE ENTRY

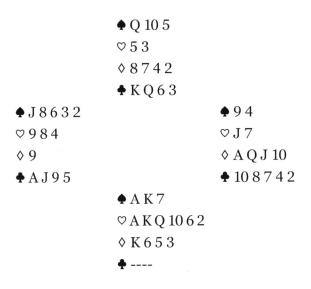

```
                    ♠ Q 10 5
                    ♡ 5 3
                    ◊ 8 7 4 2
                    ♣ K Q 6 3
   ♠ J 8 6 3 2                      ♠ 9 4
   ♡ 9 8 4                          ♡ J 7
   ◊ 9                              ◊ A Q J 10
   ♣ A J 9 5                        ♣ 10 8 7 4 2
                    ♠ A K 7
                    ♡ A K Q 10 6 2
                    ◊ K 6 5 3
                    ♣ ----
```

Contract: 4 ♡

Opening Lead: ◊ 9

The singleton diamond went to East's ace. Back came the diamond queen and West ruffed declarer's king. West exited a trump. Declarer, with two diamond losers, could go to dummy once and throw one loser on a club honor, but had no second entry. He finished down one.

Question: Was there a way to dispose of that diamond loser? A stepping stone?

Maybe with a little help from the opponents. That's what they are there for. Frank Stewart showed this theme a few years ago in one of his terrific columns.

The other declarer, after the trump return, drew trumps and cashed the spade ace. He played a spade to dummy's ten and led the club king, unblocking the spade king. West won the ace, but he was endplayed in this position:

```
                    North: ♠ Q    ♡ --        ◊ 8      ♣ Q 6 3
West: ♠ J 8 6 ♡ -- ◊ -- ♣ J 9
                    South: ♠ --   ♡ 10 6 2    ◊ 6 5    ♣ --
```

With only black cards left, West had to put declarer in the dummy. South discarded his two diamond losers on the two black queens. Thanks, Frank.

50

UNBLOCKING WITH A STEPPING STONE

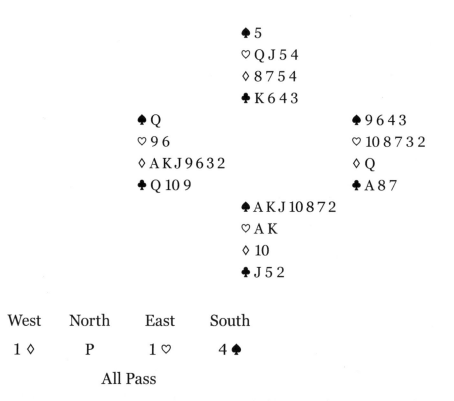

```
                        ♠ 5
                        ♡ Q J 5 4
                        ◊ 8 7 5 4
                        ♣ K 6 4 3
            ♠ Q                         ♠ 9 6 4 3
            ♡ 9 6                       ♡ 10 8 7 3 2
            ◊ A K J 9 6 3 2             ◊ Q
            ♣ Q 10 9                    ♣ A 8 7
                        ♠ A K J 10 8 7 2
                        ♡ A K
                        ◊ 10
                        ♣ J 5 2
```

West	North	East	South
1 ◊	P	1 ♡	4 ♠
	All Pass		

Opening Lead: ◊ Ace

Declarer ruffed the second diamond and drew trumps. He cashed the A-K of hearts and tried to reach dummy with a club. He lost three club tricks. Down one.

Question: Was there a way to unblock and use those nice hearts?

The other declarer was careful to ruff the second diamond with the seven. To guard against the possible club position and utilize the opponents, he drew only three rounds of trumps. After unblocking the A-K of hearts, he led the spade two:

```
    ♠ --      ♡ Q J    ◊ --     ♣ K 6 4 3
                                    ♠ 9 ♡ 10 8 ◊ -- ♣ A 8 7
    ♠ 10 8 2  ♡ --     ◊ --     ♣ J 5 2
```

The best East could do was cash the club ace, then put declarer in the dummy. Another carefully preserved two. If declarer had tried to put East in with the trump seven, East might have discarded his nine on an early trump to avoid this.

UNBLOCKING TO CREATE A STEPPING STONE ENTRY

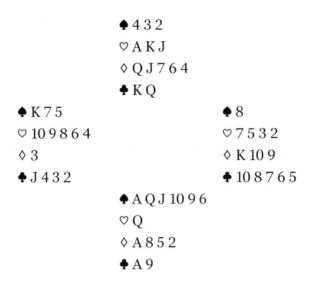

```
                    ♠ 4 3 2
                    ♡ A K J
                    ◊ Q J 7 6 4
                    ♣ K Q
    ♠ K 7 5                        ♠ 8
    ♡ 10 9 8 6 4                   ♡ 7 5 3 2
    ◊ 3                            ◊ K 10 9
    ♣ J 4 3 2                      ♣ 10 8 7 6 5
                    ♠ A Q J 10 9 6
                    ♡ Q
                    ◊ A 8 5 2
                    ♣ A 9
```

Contract: 6 ♠
Opening Lead: ♡ 10

Declarer won the opening lead in dummy and took a trump finesse. West ducked, a good play. Declarer went to dummy with a club and led another spade.

With no re-entry to dummy for a diamond finesse, he was down one.

Question: Was there a second entry to the dummy?

The second declarer just needed a little help from his friends. After the trump queen won, he went to dummy with a club and discarded the club ace on a high heart. When he led another trump and saw East show out, he played the ace of trumps and led another trump to reach this position:

                                    North: ♠ --   ♡ J   ◊ Q J 7 6 4   ♣ Q

West: ♠ -- ♡ 9 8 6 ◊ 3 ♣ J 4 3

                                    South: ♠ 10 9 6   ♡ --   ◊ A 8 5 2   ♣ --

West won the trump king, but had to put declarer in the dummy. Declarer discarded two diamonds on the winners in dummy, then took a diamond finesse.

Making six spades.

A DIFFICULT UNBLOCK: A STEPPING STONE ENTRY

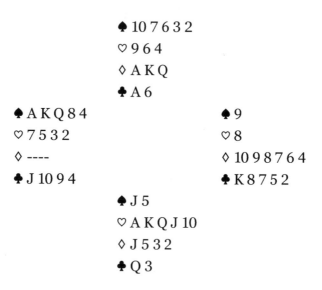

```
              ♠ 10 7 6 3 2
              ♡ 9 6 4
              ◇ A K Q
              ♣ A 6
♠ A K Q 8 4                    ♠ 9
♡ 7 5 3 2                      ♡ 8
◇ ----                         ◇ 10 9 8 7 6 4
♣ J 10 9 4                     ♣ K 8 7 5 2
              ♠ J 5
              ♡ A K Q J 10
              ◇ J 5 3 2
              ♣ Q 3
```

Contract: 4 ♡ (West overcalls spades)

Opening Lead: ♠ King

West led the king, then ace of spades, East discarding a diamond. West switched to the eight of spades, East ruffed and declarer overruffed. West's unusual lead, king then ace, suggested shortness somewhere.

Declarer drew trumps and cashed the top diamonds. With no more trumps and no way to reach the diamond jack, he had to lose two more tricks. Down one.

Question: Was there a way to reach the diamond jack, the tenth trick?

Perhaps. Play started the same at the other table, but declarer discarded the club ace while drawing trumps. After cashing the high diamonds, he led the small club from dummy in this three card ending:

North: ♠ 10 7   ♡ --   ◇ --   ♣ 6   East

                                        ♠ -- ♡ -- ◇ 10 ♣ K 8 (or ◇ 10 9 ♣ K)

South: ♠ --   ♡ --   ◇ J   ♣ Q 3

East won the club king, but he had nothing to return except a club or a diamond, putting declarer back in his hand to cash the tenth trick.

UNBLOCKING TO CREATE A STEPPING STONE ENTRY

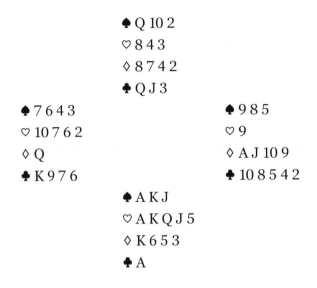

♠ Q 10 2
♡ 8 4 3
◊ 8 7 4 2
♣ Q J 3

♠ 7 6 4 3
♡ 10 7 6 2
◊ Q
♣ K 9 7 6

♠ 9 8 5
♡ 9
◊ A J 10 9
♣ 10 8 5 4 2

♠ A K J
♡ A K Q J 5
◊ K 6 5 3
♣ A

Contract: 4 ♡
Opening Lead: ◊ Queen

East won the opening lead and returned the diamond jack. West ruffed declarer's king and exited a trump. Declarer drew the rest of the trumps and lost two more diamonds. Down one.

Question: Was there a way to use some of the assets in dummy?

The Q J of clubs? The other declarer, after the same start, drew trumps and cashed the club ace. He played the spade ace, then the spade jack to the queen.

From this position he led the club queen, unblocking the spade king.

Dummy: ♠ 10 ♡ --   ◊ 8 7 ♣ Q J

West: ♠ 7 6 ♡ -- ◊ -- ♣ K 9 7

South: ♠ K   ♡ J 5 ◊ 6 5 ♣ --

West won the club king, but had to put the dummy on lead. Declarer discarded his two losing diamonds on the spade ten and club jack.

Declarer lost one diamond, one ruff, and one club. Making four hearts.

UNBLOCKING FOR A STEPPING STONE ENTRY

```
                      ♠ Q J 10 8
                      ♡ J 4
                      ◊ J 9 7 6 4
                      ♣ Q 3
         ♠ 7 6 4                      ♠ K 5 3
         ♡ 2                          ♡ Q 10 9 8 7 3
         ◊ 5 3                        ◊ 8 2
         ♣ K J 10 9 7                 ♣ 8 5
         6 2
                      ♠ A 9 2
                      ♡ A K 6 5
                      ◊ A K Q 10
                      ♣ A 4
```

Contract: 6 NT (West preempts in clubs)
Opening Lead: ◊ 5

Declarer counted only eleven tricks, assuming the spade finesse was on. Could he endplay West into leading a club? Even the spades might present entry problems. After much agony, he ended down one.

Question: Was there a road to 6 NT with all these assets?

Maybe. The other declarer played four rounds of diamonds and took two spade finesses to reach this position. Now he needed to untangle:

```
                         Dummy: ♠ 10 8  ♡ J 4      ◊ 9  ♣ Q 3
West: ♠ 7 ♡ 2 ◊ -- ♣ K J 10 9 7
                         South: ♠ A      ♡ A K 6 5  ◊ --  ♣ A 4
```

On the last high diamond, declarer unblocked the club ace. Then he cashed the ace of spades, the A-K of hearts and led a low club. West had to win and give dummy the club queen and the spade ten. Twelve tricks. Thanks to Mike Lawrence for this most interesting hand.

FINESSES,
DANGER HANDS,
AND
SECOND SUITS

UNBLOCKING FOR A FINESSE POSITION

```
                    ♠ A 10 4
                    ♡ Q 7 5 2
                    ◊ 8 6 4 3
                    ♣ 9 7
    ♠ Q 9 8 6                        ♠ K 7 5 3
    ♡ A 3                            ♡ 8 6
    ◊ K 2                            ◊ 9 7 5
    ♣ 8 6 4 3 2                      ♣ K Q 10 5
                    ♠ J 2
                    ♡ K J 10 9 4
                    ◊ A Q J 10
                    ♣ A J
```

Contract: 4 ♡

Opening Lead: ♠ 6

Declarer played low and East won the king. East returned the club king. Declarer won the ace and started the trumps. West won the ace and exited a trump. When declarer took a diamond finesse, he was down one, losing a trick in each suit.

Question: The other declarer made four hearts. Poor defense or better offense?

The first declarer went down at trick one. In the other room, the declarer unblocked the spade jack at trick one. At trick two, she won the club return with the ace and took a spade finesse, low towards dummy's ♠ A 10. When the ten won, she disposed of her club loser.

East might have been falsecarding at trick one, winning with the king from K-Q but hey, what have you got to lose?

UNBLOCKING TO PREPARE A FINESSE POSITION

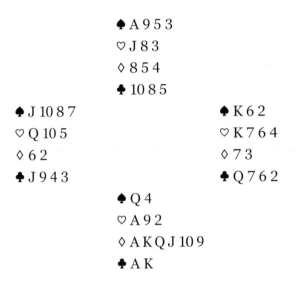

♠ A 9 5 3
♡ J 8 3
◇ 8 5 4
♣ 10 8 5

♠ J 10 8 7
♡ Q 10 5
◇ 6 2
♣ J 9 4 3

♠ K 6 2
♡ K 7 6 4
◇ 7 3
♣ Q 7 6 2

♠ Q 4
♡ A 9 2
◇ A K Q J 10 9
♣ A K

Contract: 5 ◇
Opening Lead: ♠ Jack

Declarer ducked the opening lead and won the return with the queen. He drew trumps. With no way to reach dummy's spade ace, he cashed the heart ace hoping to find a doubleton K-Q of hearts or East with a singleton honor.

He lost two hearts and one spade. Down one.

Question: Same old question, need I ask?

The other declarer in the same contract with the same opening lead, ducked trick one, but unblocked the spade queen under the ace. He was now able to later lead towards dummy's ♠ A 9 and finesse West's ten.

One heart loser was discarded on dummy's good spade. Making five diamonds.

UNBLOCKING FOR A FINESSE

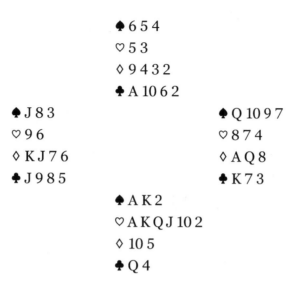

Contract: 4 ♡

Opening Lead: ♣ 5

Declarer ducked the opening lead. East won the king and switched to a diamond. The defense took two diamond tricks. Declarer had two good clubs, but could only cash one of them. He also had a late unavoidable spade loser. Down one.

Question: Was there a way to avoid the spade loser?

At the other table, declarer ducked the opening club lead but unblocked his club queen under the ace. He later led his low club towards dummy's ♣ A 10, finessing West's jack to dispose of his spade loser.

He lost two diamonds and one club.

UNBLOCKING TO SET UP RUFFING FINESSES

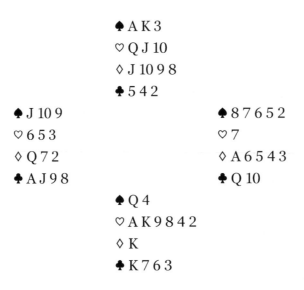

```
                    ♠ A K 3
                    ♡ Q J 10
                    ◇ J 10 9 8
                    ♣ 5 4 2
   ♠ J 10 9                        ♠ 8 7 6 5 2
   ♡ 6 5 3                         ♡ 7
   ◇ Q 7 2                         ◇ A 6 5 4 3
   ♣ A J 9 8                       ♣ Q 10
                    ♠ Q 4
                    ♡ A K 9 8 4 2
                    ◇ K
                    ♣ K 7 6 3
```

Contract: 4 ♡

Opening Lead: ♠ Jack

Declarer won the opening lead and tried the diamond jack. But East played the ace and switched to the club queen. Declarer lost three club tricks. Down one.

Question: That was quick. Any better ideas or just unlucky?

The other declarer saw much better odds. He played three rounds of spades, discarding the diamond king. Seems every hand everyone is throwing all the assets away. Then he led the diamond jack and when not covered let it ride.

West won the queen and returned a trump. Declarer took another diamond ruffing finesse. He then had two good diamonds and discarded two clubs.
He lost one diamond and two clubs.

UNBLOCKING TO CREATE A FINESSE POSITION

♠ K 7 3
♡ Q 9 2
◇ 8 4 2
♣ J 7 6 3

♠ A 8
♡ J 10 3
◇ A J 10 9 7 3
♣ 9 5

♠ 5
♡ A 8 6 5 4
◇ 6 5
♣ K Q 10 8 2

♠ Q J 10 9 6 4 2
♡ K 7
◇ K Q
♣ A 4

South	West	North	East
1 ♠	2 ◇	2 ♠	Dbl
4 ♠		All Pass	

Opening Lead: ♡ Jack

East won the opening lead and switched to the club king. Declarer won, cashed the heart king and tried to reach dummy with a trump. West won the first trump lead with the ace and cashed the diamond ace. The club return meant down one.

Question: Overbid? Assess the blame. What would you do differently?

The other declarer took advantage of East's misdefense. When East won the first trick, declarer unblocked his king of hearts. He won the club return with his ace and led his small heart towards dummy's ♡ Q 9. When the nine won, he was able to discard his club loser.

But what if East ducks the first heart? Declarer can win his king, but when he tries to draw trumps, West wins and a club shift sets up the setting tricks. If instead declarer leads a heart and finesses, the nine forces the ace, but declarer has no heart to reach dummy.

61

WHICH CARD TO UNBLOCK FOR A FINESSE?

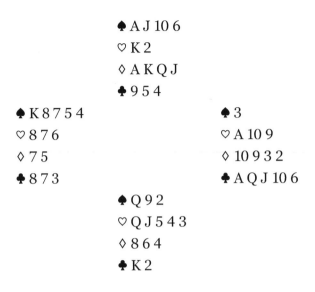

♠ A J 10 6
♡ K 2
♢ A K Q J
♣ 9 5 4

♠ K 8 7 5 4
♡ 8 7 6
♢ 7 5
♣ 8 7 3

♠ 3
♡ A 10 9
♢ 10 9 3 2
♣ A Q J 10 6

♠ Q 9 2
♡ Q J 5 4 3
♢ 8 6 4
♣ K 2

Contract: 3 NT (East opened 1 ♣)
Opening Lead: ♣ 3

East played the ten of clubs at trick one to keep communication with West. Declarer won the king, but needed the next eight tricks. Playing hearts would not be a good idea.

Needing four spade tricks, declarer led the spade queen, winning. Then he led the nine. He cashed the ace, but when the king did not fall, he was down one.

Question: What was the correct way to take four spade tricks?

The other declarer started by leading the nine, then the queen, and took four spade tricks. Leading the queen and unblocking the jack or ten does no good.

West would then cover the nine and eventually his eight would be high. Little things mean a lot.

UNBLOCKING TO CREATE A FINESSE POSITION

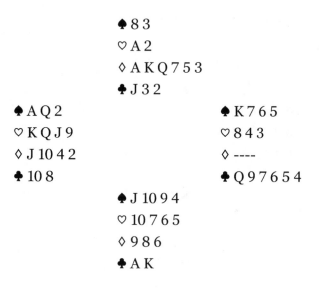

Contract: 3 NT

Opening Lead: ♡ King

Declarer won the opening lead and counted nine tricks, no problem. He played the ace of diamonds and East showed out. Declarer played low, thinking, "better East show out than West."

He came to his hand with a club and led the diamond nine, West played the ten, dummy winning. He came back and led the diamond eight, West this time played low.

The diamonds are still sitting there as you read this. Lots of undertricks. "Partner, what happened to your nine tricks?" asked North.

Question: What did happen? It looked all so simple, no?

A good declarer is a careful declarer. The other declarer unblocked the eight or nine under the diamond ace at trick two. When he reached the above crucial position, he had the ◊ 6 to lead towards dummy's ◊ Q 7, to finesse the final honor card from West's ◊ J 4.

He took the nine tricks he started with.

UNBLOCKING YOUR SECOND SUIT: DANGER HAND

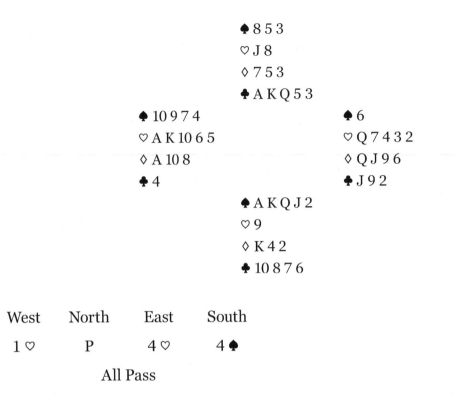

```
                    ♠ 8 5 3
                    ♡ J 8
                    ◊ 7 5 3
                    ♣ A K Q 5 3
        ♠ 10 9 7 4                   ♠ 6
        ♡ A K 10 6 5                 ♡ Q 7 4 3 2
        ◊ A 10 8                     ◊ Q J 9 6
        ♣ 4                          ♣ J 9 2
                    ♠ A K Q J 2
                    ♡ 9
                    ◊ K 4 2
                    ♣ 10 8 7 6
```

West	North	East	South
1 ♡	P	4 ♡	4 ♠
	All Pass		

Opening Lead: ♡ Ace

A typical 4 over 4 auction, a guessing game. Declarer ruffed the second heart and drew trumps. OK, time for clubs. But now declarer saw the problem. But if clubs were 2-2 or the jack was singleton....right, only in your dreams.

So after three rounds of clubs, he played a diamond to his king. Down a lot. This time North was apoplectic. "Partner, you had ten off the top, no?"

Question: Was North right? Or just blowing steam?

The other declarer foresaw the problem and also saw ten off the top. On the king of hearts at trick two by West, the safe hand on lead, declarer unblocked the clubs by discarding a club instead of ruffing.

This did not cost a trick, the diamond ace being with West. It didn't matter which three tricks were lost. Now declarer had her "ten off the top."

DUCKING TO AVOID BLOCKING

```
                      ♠ 10 5
                      ♡ 10 7 2
                      ◊ Q 10 9 7 2
                      ♣ Q J 2
   ♠ J 8 4 3                          ♠ Q 7 6 2
   ♡ A J 9 4 3                        ♡ Q
   ◊ K 3                              ◊ 8 5 4
   ♣ 10 5                            ♣ 8 7 6 4 3
                      ♠ A K 9
                      ♡ K 8 6 5
                      ◊ A J 6
                      ♣ A K 9
```

Contract: 3 NT
Opening Lead: ♡ 4

Declarer had to make a decision at trick one. If East had exactly K-x in diamonds, it was right to use dummy's one entry for a diamond finesse. Otherwise, there was the probability of blocking the diamond suit. Best to play diamonds out of his hand decided the declarer.

Perhaps hearts were 4-2 or East had the diamond king but no more hearts. He won the heart king and played ace and a diamond. West won and cashed four heart tricks. Down one.

Question: How did the other declarer made 3 NT with the same lead?

She realized she did not need a heart trick to make 3 NT. She ducked the opening lead. If East had another heart, she could not lose more than three hearts and a diamond. And since East had no more hearts, declarer was able to develop the diamonds with no problem.

FINESSE? OK BUT WHICH ONE ?

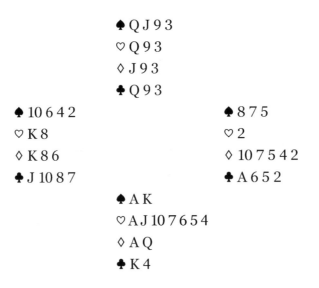

♠ Q J 9 3
♡ Q 9 3
◇ J 9 3
♣ Q 9 3

♠ 10 6 4 2   ♠ 8 7 5
♡ K 8   ♡ 2
◇ K 8 6   ◇ 10 7 5 4 2
♣ J 10 8 7   ♣ A 6 5 2

♠ A K
♡ A J 10 7 6 5 4
◇ A Q
♣ K 4

South	West	North	East
2 ♣	P	2 ◇	P
2 ♡	P	3 ♡	P
4 NT	P	5 ◇	P
5 ♡		All Pass	

Opening Lead: ♣ Jack

Declarer played low, East played the ace, declarer played low. East returned a diamond. Declarer, having had his finesses lose all day, hopefully played the queen, West won the king. West's later trump trick meant down one.

Question: Was there any road to five hearts?

At the other table, declarer was playing against two experts. Knowing you are missing two key cards, if East had the club ten, ♣ A 10 x (x), he would have ducked trick one. He knows his partner has an entry. Another club from West would give him a chance for two club tricks.

So declarer unblocked his club king under the ace. He won the diamond return, and took a club finesse towards dummy's ♣ Q 9 to discard his diamond loser.

66

UNBLOCKING TO SET UP A SECOND SUIT

```
              ♠ Q J 10 9 8
              ♡ A Q
              ◇ Q 7 6
              ♣ 9 8 2
     ♠ K 4 2                    ♠ 7 6 5 3
     ♡ K J 8 7 6 4              ♡ 10 9 5 3
     ◇ 4 2                      ◇ 5 3
     ♣ 10 4                     ♣ K Q J
              ♠ A
              ♡ 2
              ◇ A K J 10 9 8
              ♣ A 7 6 5 3
```

South	West	North	East
1 ◇	2 ♡	2 ♠	3 ♥
4 ♣	P	4 ♡	P
5 ♣	P	5 ◇	P
6 ◇		All Pass	

Opening Lead: ♡ 7

Declarer won the ace and wanted to set up the spades. With only one entry because of the trump spots, and no plan, she lost two club tricks. Down one. North was muttering something as he wrote down -100.

Question: What do you think North was muttering about?

At the other table, declarer formed a plan before he played. He took a necessary but unnecessary heart finesse at trick one, which was a favorite to win. When the heart queen held, he unblocked the spade ace on the heart ace.

He led the spade queen. When East played low, declarer discarded a club. West won, but after drawing trumps, declarer had the rest. The remaining spades in dummy were all high to discard the clubs. North wrote +1370 and smiled.

USING

THE

OPPONENTS

NO FINESSE: BLOCK THEIR SUIT

```
                    ♠ J 6 5 4 3
                    ♡ A Q
                    ◊ Q 9 2
                    ♣ J 6 4
      ♠ Q 5 2                        ♠ 10 9 6
      ♡ X X 7 6 4                    ♡ X 8
      ◊ K 6                          ◊ 7 5 3
      ♣ 10 9 2                       ♣ Q 8 7 5 3
                    ♠ A K
                    ♡ 9 5 3 2
                    ◊ A J 10 8 4
                    ♣ A K
```

Contract: 3 NT
Opening Lead: ♡ 6

Declarer # 1 finessed the queen at trick one. He later lost a diamond finesse.

Question: How did the above declarer do? What did you play at trick one?

The other declarer, # 2, won the ace at trick one and lost a diamond finesse. Let's look at four possibilities. Think about the opening lead. East rates to have an honor card. Two scenarios:

Declarer # 1. East had the heart king and returned a heart. Down one. West had the heart king. Declarer made 3 NT.
Declarer # 1 made 3 NT half the time, depending on who had the heart king.

Declarer # 2. East had the heart king, but the suit was blocked. He made 3 NT. West had the heart king. West could only cash two more tricks, The nine was a big card. He made 3 NT.
Declarer # 2, made 3 NT both times by not finessing, regardless of who had the heart king.
How did you do?

BLOCKING THE OPPONENTS' SUIT

                        ♠ Q 3
                        ♡ A Q 6 2
                        ◇ K 10 7 5
                        ♣ A Q 9

        ♠ 10 9   ♠ A K J 6 5
        ♡ 10 8 5 4 3   ♡ 7
        ◇ J 4   ◇ 9 8 6 2
        ♣ J 7 6 4   ♣ 5 3 2

                        ♠ 8 7 4 2
                        ♡ K J 9
                        ◇ A Q 3
                        ♣ K 10 8

South	West	North	East
1 ♣	P	1 ♡	P
1 NT	P	3 NT	All Pass

Opening Lead: ♠ 10

Declarer played low and East took the first five tricks. Down one. When North saw South's hand, he moaned and asked, "Didn't you read Dr J's book?"

Question: What was North referring to? Good lead? What could declarer do?

Little things mean a lot. Yes, a different lead and declarer had a lot of tricks. But the other declarer received the same opening lead and played the queen. What could East do?

If he played spades from the top, South's eight was good. If East returned a low spade, West would win the nine, but would not have another spade. Making 3 NT.

BLOCKING THE OPPONENTS' SUIT

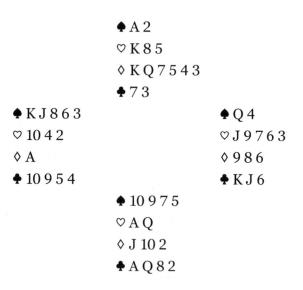

Contract: 3 NT

Opening Lead: ♠ 6

Declarer played low and East won the queen. East returned a spade. Declarer had to play diamonds and West took three more spade tricks. Down one.

North gave South her copy of my book and said, "Don't call me again until you have read this."

Question: How should declarer have played?

The other declarer gave more thought to the opening lead. If West had five spades, were they ♠ K Q J x x? Unlikely.

More likely, West had one honor, probably a doubleton. So declarer played the spade ace at trick one.

The defense was helpless. If East unblocked his queen, declarer would have a second stopper. When West won the ace of diamonds, if he led low, East would win but have no more spades. If he led high, declarer had a second stopper.

BLOCKING THE OPPONENTS' SUIT

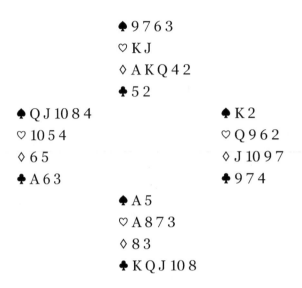

♠ 9 7 6 3
♡ K J
◇ A K Q 4 2
♣ 5 2

♠ Q J 10 8 4
♡ 10 5 4
◇ 6 5
♣ A 6 3

♠ K 2
♡ Q 9 6 2
◇ J 10 9 7
♣ 9 7 4

♠ A 5
♡ A 8 7 3
◇ 8 3
♣ K Q J 10 8

Contract: 3 NT
Opening Lead: ♠ Queen

Declarer ducked the opening lead, perhaps out of habit. West continued with a low spade, king, ace. When West won the club ace, declarer was down one.

Question: How should declarer have played?

The other declarer gave more thought to the opening lead. If West had a five card suit like ♠ Q J 10 x x, then East had ♠ K x. With the nine in dummy, East could not afford to overtake with the king.

So this declarer won the first trick and the suit was blocked. After knocking out the club ace, the defenders could only take one more spade trick.

BLOCKING THE OPPONENTS' SUIT

```
                        ♠ Q 10 4
                        ♡ 8 7 2
                        ◇ J 7 6 5 2
                        ♣ K Q
        ♠ 9 3                           ♠ A J 8 6 5
        ♡ 10 9 5 4                      ♡ Q J 3
        ◇ 10 4 3                        ◇ K 9 8
        ♣ A 8 4 3                       ♣ 6 5
                        ♠ K 7 2
                        ♡ A K 6
                        ◇ A Q
                        ♣ J 10 9 7 2
```

West	North	East	South
P	P	1♠	1 NT
P	3 NT		All Pass

Opening Lead: ♠ 9

Declarer won the first spade with his king. He led a club and was surprised to see West win the ace. Another spade continuation meant four spade tricks for East.

Down one.

Question: Was there a better game plan?

Declarer knew the spade layout. East had ♠ A J x x x. If declarer played the queen at trick one, East was helpless. If East won the ace, he could not continue the suit or the ten in dummy would win a trick. If East played low, declarer had a second stopper.

The suit was effectively blocked.

BLOCKING THE OPPONENTS' SUIT

```
                    ♠ A 5 2
                    ♡ Q J 6
                    ◇ A 8 5 3
                    ♣ Q 7 2
     ♠ K 10 8 6 3                      ♠ Q 9
     ♡ K 5 2                           ♡ 8 7 4
     ◇ 10 7                            ◇ Q J 9 2
     ♣ J 9 4                           ♣ 10 8 6 3
                    ♠ J 7 4
                    ♡ A 10 9 3
                    ◇ K 6 4
                    ♣ A K 5
```

Contract: 3 NT

Opening Lead: ♠ 6

Declarer played low at trick one, perhaps from habit. East won and returned a spade. Declarer had no choice but to take a heart finesse. West won and cashed three spade tricks. Down one.

Question: How should declarer have played? What was the winning 'clue'?

The other declarer played the spade ace at trick one. Why? He gave more thought to the opening lead. If spades were 4-3, fine. If West was leading from five, what was the layout? Only if West had led from K Q x x x was it right to duck.

More likely the top two honors were divided. If West had K Q 10 x x x, he probably would have led the king. When declarer played the ace, it would not help for East to unblock the queen.

Declarer had nine tricks after the heart finesse.

BLOCKING THE OPPONENTS' SUIT

         ♠ K 7 2
         ♡ Q J 8 3
         ◊ 8 6
         ♣ J 9 8 4

♠ 8 5   ♠ 10 9 6 3
♡ 10 7 4   ♡ 9 6 2
◊ A 9 4 3 2   ◊ K J 10
♣ Q 10 5   ♣ K 7 3

         ♠ A Q J 4
         ♡ A K 5
         ◊ Q 7 5
         ♣ A 6 2

Contract: 3 NT
Opening Lead: ◊ 3

East won the diamond king and returned the jack. Like most, declarer ducked, hoping East started with K J doubleton. East continued with the ten. Down one.

Question: Why did the other declarer play the queen at trick two?

Again, think about the opening lead. The three does not suggest a six card suit. It can be fourth best only from a four or five card suit. If the three is fourth best, the Rule of Eleven says East has three diamonds. Therefore, the best chance is to cover and hope to block the suit.

There are situations like these where leading fourth best helps declarer more than partner. Leading the lowest, the two, is often best.

BLOCKING THEIR SUIT FROM THE OTHER SIDE

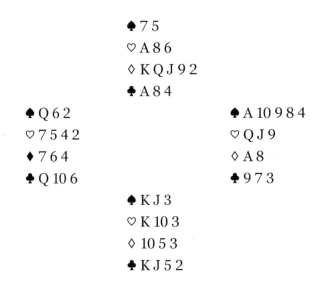

```
                        ♠ 7 5
                        ♡ A 8 6
                        ◊ K Q J 9 2
                        ♣ A 8 4
        ♠ Q 6 2                        ♠ A 10 9 8 4
        ♡ 7 5 4 2                      ♡ Q J 9
        ♦ 7 6 4                        ◊ A 8
        ♣ Q 10 6                       ♣ 9 7 3
                        ♠ K J 3
                        ♡ K 10 3
                        ◊ 10 5 3
                        ♣ K J 5 2
```

North	East	South	West
1 ◊	1 ♠	2 NT	P
3 NT		All Pass	

Opening Lead: ♠ 2

East won the spade ace and returned the ten. Declarer played the jack. Down one. That was quick.

Question: What should declarer have been thinking about at trick two?

The other declarer played the spade king, blocking the suit. The most likely original holding for West was ♠ Q x x. East might have done better returning the eight or nine. Then declarer would have had more of a guess. West might have started with ♠ 10 x x.

A similar situation:

```
                              x
              J x x                     A K x x
                      Q 10 x x
```

76

BLOCKING THE OPPONENTS' SUIT BY DUCKING

```
                    ♠ A K
                    ♡ J 6 5 4 3
                    ◇ A K J
                    ♣ Q 10 6
      ♠ J 10 9 6                      ♠ 8 4 3
      ♡ A K 9                         ♡ Q 8 7 2
      ◇ 9 6 5 3                       ◇ 10 4
      ♣ K 7                           ♣ 9 8 4 3
                    ♠ Q 7 5 2
                    ♡ 10
                    ◇ Q 8 7 2
                    ♣ A J 5 2
```

Contract: 3 NT
Opening Lead: ♠ Jack

With eight top tricks, declarer won the opening lead and took a club finesse. West won and switched to the heart king. East played an encouraging eight so West continued with the heart ace, then the nine.

Declarer covered with the jack. The defense took four heart tricks. Down one.

Question: Was the contract doomed after the heart switch?

The other declarer was paying closer attention to what was going on in the heart suit. He was quite sure East had the queen from the carding so far. If East also had the seven, playing the jack was giving up.

He ducked the heart nine. It won the trick as East followed with the seven, but East could not afford to overtake. The suit was blocked. Making 3 NT.

SUIT BLOCKED? LET THE OPPONENTS UNBLOCK IT

```
                        ♠ 8 7 4 3
                        ♡ 6 5
                        ◊ A K Q 3 2
                        ♣ Q 9
        ♠ J 9 6 2                       ♠ Q 10 5
        ♡ A J 3                         ♡ 10 9 8 7 4
        ◊ J 8 4                         ◊ 5
        ♣ J 8 6                         ♣ K 7 4 2
                        ♠ A K
                        ♡ K Q 2
                        ◊ 10 9 7 6
                        ♣ A 10 5 3
```

Contract: 3 NT
Opening Lead: ♠ 2

Declarer at first counted plenty of tricks. Knock out the heart ace, then two spades, one heart, five diamonds, and at least one club. What's the problem? He soon found out when he cashed the A-K of diamonds and the suit divided 3-1.

There was no recovery. He finished with eight tricks, down one.

Question: Was there a way to overcome the 3-1 split and the suit blockage?

Probably. The other declarer cashed one round of diamonds to see if the jack would fall. Then he cashed the other top spade and played another high diamond. East showed out. But trusting the opening lead to be from a four card suit, he led a spade and discarded a diamond.

The defense was helpless. After they cashed their spade tricks, declarer still had a diamond to reach dummy and the suit was no longer blocked.

GIVE THE OPPONENTS A CHANCE TO GO WRONG

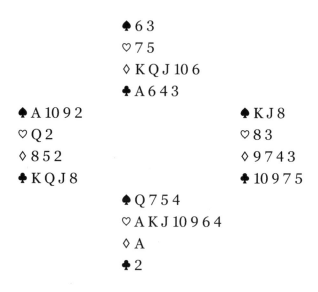

♠ 6 3
♡ 7 5
◇ K Q J 10 6
♣ A 6 4 3

♠ A 10 9 2
♡ Q 2
◇ 8 5 2
♣ K Q J 8

♠ K J 8
♡ 8 3
◇ 9 7 4 3
♣ 10 9 7 5

♠ Q 7 5 4
♡ A K J 10 9 6 4
◇ A
♣ 2

Contract: 4 ♡

Opening Lead: ♣ King

Declarer won the opening lead. With the diamonds blocked, he tried to ruff spades in dummy. The defenders won the first two spades and played trumps each time.

Declarer lost four spade tricks. Down one.

Question. How did the other declarer make four hearts? Brain dead opponents?

The other declarer, seeing the opponents were not on life support, correctly reasoned trying to ruff spades would fail as above. She casually ducked the opening lead. The opponents were not brain dead, but on the other hand, West made the normal play of continuing with the club queen.

Declarer unblocked his diamond ace on the club ace and started playing high diamonds, discarding spades. Since diamonds were 4-3, he discarded all his spades as West finally ruffed in. He lost one club and one heart.

TEMPTING THE OPPONENTS TO HELP YOU

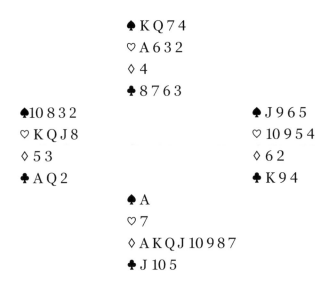

<pre>
                    ♠ K Q 7 4
                    ♡ A 6 3 2
                    ◊ 4
                    ♣ 8 7 6 3
    ♠10 8 3 2   ♠ J 9 6 5
    ♡ K Q J 8   ♡ 10 9 5 4
    ◊ 5 3   ◊ 6 2
    ♣ A Q 2   ♣ K 9 4
                    ♠ A
                    ♡ 7
                    ◊ A K Q J 10 9 8 7
                    ♣ J 10 5
</pre>

West	North	East	South
1 ♣	P	1 ♡	5 ◊
	All Pass		

Opening Lead: ♡ King

The opening lead had taken away declarer's entry to the good spades. Declarer won the heart ace and drew trumps. He lost the three obvious club tricks.

Down one. "Partner, did you already forget the previous hand?" moaned North.

Question: Do you remember the one we just did? Coincidentally_____

Eddie Kantar showed this hand recently ("ACBL Bulletin," February, 2021), the twin cousin of the previous hand. You just need a little help from your friends.
   The other declarer smoothly (emphasis smoothly), ducked the opening lead. West continued with the heart queen. Declarer's problem was solved.

He unblocked the spade ace under the heart ace and discarded two club losers on the high spades. Making five diamonds, losing one heart and one club.
   Thanks, Eddie !

BLOCKED SUIT? HOPE FOR A DEFENSIVE ERROR

```
                        ♠ 6
                        ♡ 8 5 2
                        ◇ 10 5
                        ♣ A 10 9 8 7 5 3
        ♠ Q 10                           ♠ K 9 8 7 3
        ♡ J 10 3                         ♡ Q 9 6
        ◇ A J 9 7 3 2                    ◇ Q 8 6
        ♣ K 2                            ♣ 6 4
                        ♠ A J 5 4 2
                        ♡ A K 7 4
                        ◇ K 4
                        ♣ Q J
```

North	East	South	West
3 ♣	P	3 NT	All Pass

Opening Lead: ◇ 7

Declarer won the diamond king and led the club queen. West played the king. South had no recourse. There was no way to use the club suit. Down a few.

Question: Was there any hope for 3 NT?

The other declarer won the diamond king and considered his options. Not many. Even a singleton king would not be enough. But he led the jack of clubs, a little less likely to be covered.

If you were West, would you play the king and block declarer's suit?

GETTING HELP FROM THE OPPONENTS

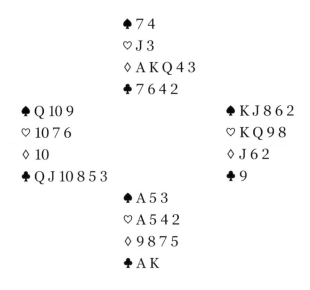

```
                      ♠ 7 4
                      ♡ J 3
                      ◇ A K Q 4 3
                      ♣ 7 6 4 2
        ♠ Q 10 9                    ♠ K J 8 6 2
        ♡ 10 7 6                    ♡ K Q 9 8
        ◇ 10                        ◇ J 6 2
        ♣ Q J 10 8 5 3              ♣ 9
                      ♠ A 5 3
                      ♡ A 5 4 2
                      ◇ 9 8 7 5
                      ♣ A K
```

Contract: 3 NT
Opening Lead: ♣ Queen

Declarer won the opening lead and played a diamond. If diamonds were 2-2, the blocked suit was no problem. But when the diamond suit divided 3-1, there was no recovery. He took his seven top tricks. Down two.

Question: Is there a way to unblock the diamonds?

The other declarer won the opening club lead and cashed the club king too. Then he played a diamond to dummy and led another club, discarding a blocking diamond.

West had no effective defense. He could cash three clubs and declarer had the rest, or he could switch and declarer had nine tricks. The diamonds were unblocked.

UNBLOCKING WITH HELP FROM THE OPPONENTS

```
                    ♠ 6 5
                    ♡ 10 5
                    ◊ A 6 4 2
                    ♣ A Q 5 4 2
   ♠ J 8 3                        ♠ Q 9 7 4
   ♡ K Q 7                        ♡ 9 8 6 4 3
   ◊ K Q J 9 5 3                  ◊ 7
   ♣ 7                            ♣ J 10 3
                    ♠ A K 10 2
                    ♡ A J 2
                    ◊ 10 8
                    ♣ K 9 8 6
```

Contract: 3 NT
Opening Lead: ◊ King

Declarer counted nine tricks and won the opening lead. He cashed the top three clubs, then realized the problem. Nine had become eight with no way back to the last club.

The clubs were tangled. Down one.

Question: To untangle, remember "I Get By With A Little Help From My Friends."

Don't be ashamed to ask for a little help. The other declarer ducked the first two rounds of diamonds. On the third round, he discarded an obstructing club.

And if the opponents switched instead of continuing diamonds? The ace of diamonds is always there; declarer would have to play a second low diamond himself.

HANDLING

BAD

SPLITS

UNBLOCKING WHEN SUITS BREAK BADLY

```
                    ♠ 5 2
                    ♡ J 6 3 2
                    ◊ Q 7
                    ♣ A K Q 10 6
        ♠ 10 9 8                    ♠ Q J 7 6 3
        ♡ 10 5                      ♡ K Q 9 7
        ◊ J 8 6                     ◊ K 9 5 3
        ♣ J 9 5 4 2                 ♣ ----
                    ♠ A K 4
                    ♡ A 8 4
                    ◊ A 10 4 2
                    ♣ 8 7 3
```

North	East	South	West
1 ♣	Dbl	Rdbl	P
P	1 ♠	3NT	All Pass

Opening Lead: ♠ 10

Declarer won the opening lead and led a low club to dummy. East showed out. When he led the club seven, West covered. But when he next led the eight, West ducked and the suit was blocked. Declarer took only four club tricks, eight tricks in all. Down one.

Question: Would you have seen the solution in time? Starting clubs with the_ ?

At the other table, the declarer, just from experience and good technical habits, started the clubs by leading the seven. Subsequently, he was able to lead the eight, then the three later and take five club tricks. Making 3 NT.

Yes, on the run of even four clubs, East is under pressure and some declarers may survive on a squeeze.

4/1 SPLIT; HOW NOT TO BLOCK YOURSELF

```
                    ♠ 8 4
                    ♡ Q 4
                    ◇ A K 9 8 2
                    ♣ 9 8 6 2
  ♠ Q 9                            ♠ J 10 7 6 3
  ♡ K J 10 5 3                     ♡ A 9
  ◇ J 7 6 4                        ◇ 5
  ♣ 10 5                           ♣ K J 7 4 3
                    ♠ A K 5 2
                    ♡ 8 7 6 2
                    ◇ Q 10 3
                    ♣ A Q
```

Contract: 3 NT
Opening Lead: ♡ Jack

Declarer covered with the queen, East won the ace and returned the nine. West could not overtake. East shifted to the four of clubs. Declarer needed two club tricks so he took a finesse, winning. It was time for the diamonds.

If East had four diamonds to the jack, declarer could not win five diamond tricks. He led the three to the ace and low back to his queen. East showed out. When he led the ten, West played low. The suit was blocked. Down one.

Question: How would you have handled the diamond suit?

The other declarer started with the ten to the ace, then back to his queen. He now had a finesse position, the ◇ K 9 in dummy, West with ◇ J 7, and the three in his hand. He took five diamonds, two clubs, and two spades. Making 3 NT.

"I knew I should have led a low heart," moaned West, "like Dr J always tells me."

FARSIGHTED UNBLOCKING TO HANDLE A 4-0 SPLIT

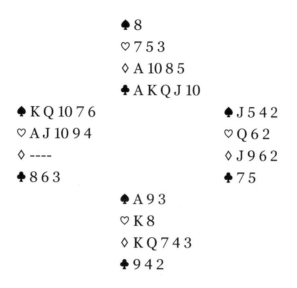

♠ 8
♡ 7 5 3
◇ A 10 8 5
♣ A K Q J 10

♠ K Q 10 7 6
♡ A J 10 9 4
◇ ----
♣ 8 6 3

♠ J 5 4 2
♡ Q 6 2
◇ J 9 6 2
♣ 7 5

♠ A 9 3
♡ K 8
◇ K Q 7 4 3
♣ 9 4 2

Contract: 6 ◇ (West bid Michaels, Majors)
Opening Lead: ♠ King

Declarer won the opening lead and ruffed a spade. He cashed the diamond ace, then led the diamond ten. East covered with the jack, declarer won the queen. He ruffed his last spade. Unable to reach his hand, declarer started the clubs. East ruffed the third club and led a heart. Declarer finished down two.

North was shaking her head, writing -200, thinking "Cold slam."

Question: Unlucky? Preventable? Poor technique? Was North right?

At the other table, declarer considered the strong possibility of a 4-0 trump split based on the bidding. So he unblocked the diamonds by ruffing the first spade with dummy's eight of diamonds. When he cashed the ace and West showed out, his farsighted thinking had paid off.

He led the diamond ten, jack, queen. He went to dummy with a club and led the diamond five. North wrote + 1370.

UNBLOCKING TO HANDLE BAD SPLITS

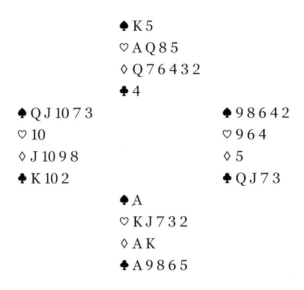

♠ K 5
♡ A Q 8 5
◊ Q 7 6 4 3 2
♣ 4

♠ Q J 10 7 3
♡ 10
◊ J 10 9 8
♣ K 10 2

♠ 9 8 6 4 2
♡ 9 6 4
◊ 5
♣ Q J 7 3

♠ A
♡ K J 7 3 2
◊ A K
♣ A 9 8 6 5

Contract: 7 ♡

Opening Lead: ♠ Queen

Declarer, optimistic that all suits would behave, won the spade ace and cashed the A-K of trumps. When West showed out, declarer needed the second suit to behave. He cashed the A-K of diamonds, but East ruffed the second round.

Down one. "Why do these things happen to me?" moaned South. North grimaced as he wrote --100.

Question: Do you remember the Matt Denis tune, "Everything Happens To Me"?

The other declarer wanted to protect herself against bad splits; 3-1 trumps and/or 4-1 diamonds. She won the spade ace, cashed the heart king and the ace of diamonds. She went to dummy with the heart ace. When West showed out, she cashed the spade king, unblocking the diamond king.

She continued with a low diamond. East could not gain by ruffing. Declarer ruffed, drew the last trump with the queen, and ruffed one more diamond. The dummy was now good after the club ace. North smiled and wrote + 2210.

UNBLOCKING WHEN TRUMPS ARE 4/1

```
                    ♠ K J 8 4
                    ♡ K 5
                    ◇ A K 5 4 2
                    ♣ K 7
        ♠ 9                           ♠ A 10 6 5
        ♡ A 10 9 8 7 4                ♡ 6 3
        ◇ Q J 8                       ◇ 9 7
        ♣ J 9 3                       ♣ Q 10 8 6 4
                    ♠ Q 7 3 2
                    ♡ Q J 2
                    ◇ 10 6 3
                    ♣ A 5 2
```

Contract: 4 ♠ (West overcalls hearts)

Opening Lead: ♡ Ace

Declarer needed to hold his trump losers to one. He wanted to start trumps from his hand, so he unblocked the heart king at trick one. He won the second heart in hand and led a trump. East won and played a club to the king. West showed out on the trump jack.

Declarer played the club to his ace and ruffed a club low. He played dummy's last trump, the eight, East played low.

Declarer could not get back to his hand and had to play diamonds. West won the third diamond and gave East a heart ruff. Down one.

Question: How could you have arranged to draw the trumps?

Play was fine until declarer wanted to ruff his club. The trump position was:

```
        ♠ 8 4
                    ♠ 10 6
        ♠ Q 7
```

If declarer had ruffed with the eight instead of the four, he could have drawn trumps, coming back to his hand by finessing East's ten.

89

OFFENSE: LITTLE OF THIS AND THAT

USING ONE BLOCKED SUIT TO UNTANGLE THE OTHER

```
                        ♠ K Q 7
                        ♡ 8 6 4
                        ◊ J 7 2
                        ♣ A K J 5
        ♠ A 5                          ♠ 10 9 8 2
        ♡ J 10 9 3                     ♡ K 7 5 2
        ◊ A Q 8 5                      ◊ 10 6 3
        ♣ 9 7 4                        ♣ 10 8
                        ♠ J 6 4 3
                        ♡ A Q
                        ◊ K 9 4
                        ♣ Q 6 3 2
```

Contract: 3 NT

Opening Lead: ♡ Jack

Declarer won the heart queen and led a low spade to the king. He needed two more spade tricks. If spades were 3-3, he could lead the queen, but it would be better to lead towards the queen in case West now had the bare spade ace.

Declarer played a club to his queen and led a spade. West won the ace and returned a heart. Declarer had ♠ J 6 opposite ♠ Q, but he had no way back to his hand to cash the last spade. Only eight tricks.

Down one.

Question: How would you have improved declarer's transportation?

The other declarer started the same, but after winning the first spade, he cashed the A-K of clubs. When both followed, he knew he had two club entries to his hand to unblock the good queen and jack of spades. He would play the club jack to the queen and the club five to the six.

He had nine tricks. Three spades, two hearts, and four clubs.

BLOCK YOUR OWN SUIT TO MAXIMIZE CHANCES

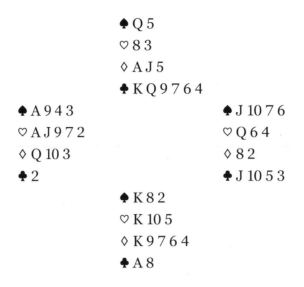

```
                    ♠ Q 5
                    ♡ 8 3
                    ◇ A J 5
                    ♣ K Q 9 7 6 4
    ♠ A 9 4 3                      ♠ J 10 7 6
    ♡ A J 9 7 2                    ♡ Q 6 4
    ◇ Q 10 3                       ◇ 8 2
    ♣ 2                            ♣ J 10 5 3
                    ♠ K 8 2
                    ♡ K 10 5
                    ◇ K 9 7 6 4
                    ♣ A 8
```

Contract: 3 NT
Opening Lead: ♡ 7

Declarer won the opening lead with the heart king. Declarer saw two good chances: either 3-2 clubs, or 3-2 diamonds with West having the queen. Having been taught to lead honor from the short side to avoid blocking a suit, declarer played to the ace of clubs first, then a club to dummy's king. West showed out.

OK, Plan B. But to execute Plan B, declarer wanted to lead low to the jack of diamonds and was in the dummy. And now he was going to block this suit trying to finesse the queen of diamonds. 3 NT was not in the cards now.

Question: How would you have made best use of your chances?

The other declarer also correctly tried clubs first but the 'wrong' way. He led low to dummy, then back to his ace blocking the suit. But if clubs were 3-2, he had an entry. And if not, he was in the correct hand to try the diamonds.

Plan B, 3-2 diamonds with the queen onside was successful. Making 3 NT.

A FREE FINESSE ? SIMPLE UNBLOCK

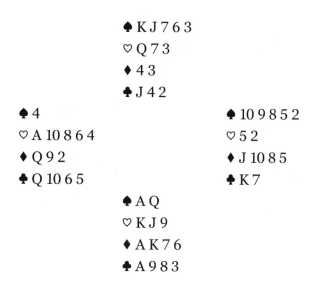

```
              ♠ K J 7 6 3
              ♡ Q 7 3
              ♦ 4 3
              ♣ J 4 2
♠ 4                          ♠ 10 9 8 5 2
♡ A 10 8 6 4                 ♡ 5 2
♦ Q 9 2                      ♦ J 10 8 5
♣ Q 10 6 5                   ♣ K 7
              ♠ A Q
              ♡ K J 9
              ♦ A K 7 6
              ♣ A 9 8 3
```

Contract: 3 NT

Opening Lead: ♡ 6

Declarer won the opening lead with the nine, perhaps too quickly. He played the A-Q of spades, but West showed out, so overtaking was not an option. He needed four spade tricks, not three. He needed to reach dummy, but the only entry was the heart queen.

If he led the heart jack, West would win the ace and block the suit. If he led the king, West would duck. He tried the jack, West won. No 3 NT for this declarer.

Question: How would you have made your way back to dummy?

The other declarer used the Rule of Eleven. West was marked with all the hearts higher than the six. The heart queen was a sure entry as long as declarer kept two cards lower than the queen.

He won trick one with the king of hearts. West could not prevent him from later reaching dummy and the good spades.

NO FINESSE, LISTEN TO THE BIDDING

♠ A 10 6 5 4
♡ Q 7 6
◊ A Q 7
♣ 9 2

♠ Q 3
♡ 4 2
◊ J 10 9 8 5 4
♣ A 10 4

♠ K J 9
♡ 9 5 3
◊ K 3
♣ 8 7 6 5 3

♠ 8 7 2
♡ A K J 10 8
◊ 6 2
♣ K Q J

West	North	East	South
2 ◊	P	P	2 ♡
P	4 ♡	All Pass	

Opening Lead: ◊ Jack

Declarer was facing four possible losers: Two spades, one diamond, and one club. She took a diamond finesse at trick one. East won the king and returned the suit. The four losers came true. Down one.

Question: How did declarer at the other table make four hearts?

The diamond finesse can wait. There is more important work to be done. Win the diamond ace and draw trumps. Now lead a diamond.

If West plays the king, the queen is good to discard a spade loser. If West plays low, duck. East is most likely down to a singleton (king?) and again the queen is good for a discard.

DECLARER UNBLOCKS

```
              ♠ 8 5
              ♡ Q 7 6 4
              ◊ A K 8 6 4 3
              ♣ 6
♠ A Q 9 4                    ♠ J 7 6 3
♡ 10                         ♡ J 9 8 3 2
◊ Q J 10 5                   ◊ 7
♣ Q 10 7 3                   ♣ 9 5 4
              ♠ K 10 2
              ♡ A K 5
              ◊ 9 2
              ♣ A K J 8 2
```

Contract: 3 NT
Opening Lead: ◊ Queen

Declarer considered ducking but did not want a spade switch. He won the opening lead with the ace, East followed with the seven. He came to his hand with a heart and led the diamond nine. West played low, a very good play.

Declarer won the king. He led another diamond, but with only one dummy entry, declarer could not both set up and use the long diamonds. He finished with eight tricks. Down one.

Question: Where did the other declarer find a ninth trick?

Little things mean a lot. At trick one, when West led a diamond, declarer won but she played the nine from her hand. Look at the difference. When she played the diamond two, West had to cover. Declarer won and played the eight. The eight forced out the other high honor. She had nine tricks.

UNBLOCK: DISCARD MOST OF THE HIGH CARDS

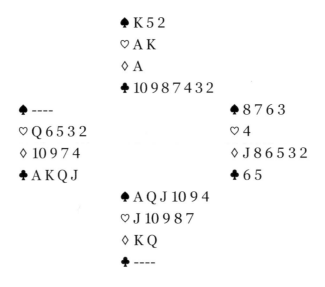

♠ K 5 2
♥ A K
♦ A
♣ 10 9 8 7 4 3 2

♠ ----
♥ Q 6 5 3 2
♦ 10 9 7 4
♣ A K Q J

♠ 8 7 6 3
♥ 4
♦ J 8 6 5 3 2
♣ 6 5

♠ A Q J 10 9 4
♥ J 10 9 8 7
♦ K Q
♣ ----

Contract: 6 ♠

Opening Lead: ♣ Ace

Declarer ruffed the opening lead. "Maybe missed a grand, partner," said South, and confidently played the ace of trumps. "Just try to make six," thought North, having heard this before. When West showed out, play slowed.

Declarer played the A-K of hearts, but East ruffed the second heart and returned a trump. Declarer played another heart, but West did not cover. Declarer was finished. If he ruffed high, he had a late heart loser. If he didn't ruff, East would ruff. Down one.

Question: Was there a way to untangle all these assets?

Too many assets. The other declarer discarded them. He ruffed the opening lead and drew trumps. On the fourth round of trumps, he discarded dummy's ace of diamonds. He cashed the K-Q of diamonds, discarding the A-K of hearts from dummy. The opponents were welcome to the heart queen.

Twelve tricks in his own hand, who needs all those high ones in the dummy.

UNBLOCKING YOUR SUIT BY
HOLDING OFF IN ANOTHER

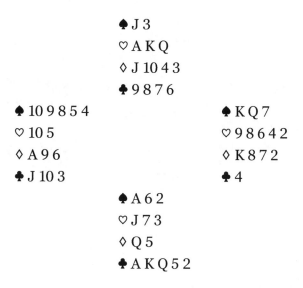

♠ J 3
♡ A K Q
◇ J 10 4 3
♣ 9 8 7 6

♠ 10 9 8 5 4
♡ 10 5
◇ A 9 6
♣ J 10 3

♠ K Q 7
♡ 9 8 6 4 2
◇ K 8 7 2
♣ 4

♠ A 6 2
♡ J 7 3
◇ Q 5
♣ A K Q 5 2

Contract: 3 NT
Opening Lead: ♠ 10

Declarer counted nine tricks too quickly and played the spade ace. When he cashed the top three clubs, the problem finally became apparent.

There was no recovery. Down one.

Question: How did the declarer in the other room overcome the club blockage?

By seeing the problem in advance, he ducked the opening lead. When the opponents continued spades, he ducked again. When he won the third spade, he discarded a high club from dummy. Problem solved.

And if the opponents had discontinued playing spades? Declarer could play them himself, the same way.

UNBLOCK WHAT? TOO EARLY TO DECIDE

```
                      ♠ A J 5 3
                      ♡ 8 6 3
                      ◊ K J 4
                      ♣ 4 3 2
        ♠ K Q 9 8 6 4                  ♠ 10 7 2
        ♡ A Q 2                        ♡ J 7 5 4
        ◊ Q                            ◊ 9
        ♣ K 9 7                        ♣ J 10 8 6 5
                      ♠ ----
                      ♡ K 10 9
                      ◊ A 10 8 7 6 5 3 2
                      ♣ A Q
```

South	West	North	East
1 ◊	1 ♠	1 NT	P
5 ◊		All Pass	

Opening Lead: ♠ King

Declarer won the spade ace, discarding a heart. He took a club finesse. West won and returned a trump. Declarer won and took a heart finesse. Down one.

West asked, "Didn't you read Dr J's book about finesses being the last resort?"

Question: How did the other declarer try to avoid these early finesses?

At trick one, the other declarer did not know what he wanted to throw on the spade ace so he ruffed in hand. He led a trump to the board and played a heart. If East played the ace, the hand was over. Otherwise, he just planned to cover East's card. West would be endplayed in three suits.

Now he would know what to use the spade ace for. Had dummy not had the spade jack, he would have thrown the club queen and taken two heart finesses, low to the nine, then low to the ten playing for East to have the queen or jack.

DON'T BLOCK YOURSELF

```
                        ♠ 7 3
                        ♡ K J 10 9 2
                        ◇ J 10 2
                        ♣ K J 3
        ♠ K 4 2                          ♠ Q J 8 6 5
        ♡ 7 4                            ♡ A 8 5 3
        ◇ 9 7 6 5 4                      ◇ K 8
        ♣ 10 8 2                         ♣ Q 9
                        ♠ A 10 9
                        ♡ Q 6
                        ◇ A Q 3
                        ♣ A 7 6 5 4
```

East	South	West	North
1 ♠	1 NT	P	2 ◇*	* Transfer to hearts
P	2 ♡	P	3 NT
	All Pass		

Opening Lead: ♠ 2

Declarer won the third round of spades, discarding a diamond. Then he considered his options. From the bidding, it was likely East had the heart ace. To try for eight minor tricks, he played the ace, then king of clubs.

First wish granted, the queen of clubs fell. He cashed the club jack and led the diamond jack. When East covered, declarer was left with ◇ Q 3 facing ◇ 10.

No three diamond tricks for this declarer. Down one,

Question: How can you untangle these tricks and not block yourself?

The other declarer started the same, but on the third spade discarded a heart, a powerful but useless suit. The hearts might just as well have been all deuces. But now he had three diamonds, five clubs, and the spade ace. Nine tricks.

UNBLOCKING TO PLAY FOR BETTER ODDS

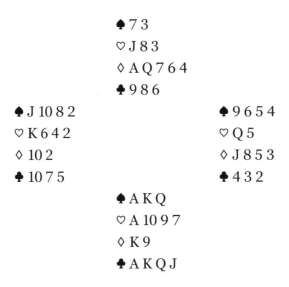

♠ 7 3
♡ J 8 3
◇ A Q 7 6 4
♣ 9 8 6

♠ J 10 8 2
♡ K 6 4 2
◇ 10 2
♣ 10 7 5

♠ 9 6 5 4
♡ Q 5
◇ J 8 5 3
♣ 4 3 2

♠ A K Q
♡ A 10 9 7
◇ K 9
♣ A K Q J

Contract: 6 NT

Opening Lead: ♠ Jack

Declarer had a choice: play for 3-3 diamonds and thirteen tricks, or something else. He won the opening lead and cashed the diamond king. He led a diamond to dummy's ace and then played the diamond queen. When West showed out, he finished with eleven tricks. - 50

"Did you think we were in seven no trump?" sarcastically asked North.

Question: Unlucky or was there a better play for six no trump?

What was the old chewing gum commercial about double your pleasure or something like that? How about double your odds? The odds of a 3-3 diamond split are about 33%.

The other declarer took a 75% line of play. He unblocked the diamonds, using them as entries to take two heart finesses. He played for split honors, or both honors with East, a 75% play. Making 6 NT.

The second half of the gum commercial was "double your fun." Sounds like + 990.

UNBLOCKING: ONE SUIT WIDE OPEN BUT

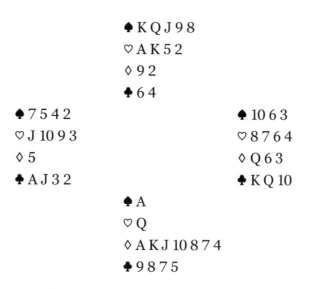

♠ K Q J 9 8
♡ A K 5 2
◇ 9 2
♣ 6 4

♠ 7 5 4 2
♡ J 10 9 3
◇ 5
♣ A J 3 2

♠ 10 6 3
♡ 8 7 6 4
◇ Q 6 3
♣ K Q 10

♠ A
♡ Q
◇ A K J 10 8 7 4
♣ 9 8 7 5

Contract: 3 NT
Opening Lead: ♡ Jack

With the major suits blocked, declarer won the heart queen, cashed the spade ace, and then hoped the diamonds would be good for seven more tricks. East won the third diamond and switched to a club. Down one, sad with so many tricks sitting in the dummy.

"Sorry partner," said South. "I couldn't untangle the tricks." North muttered something unprintable under her breath and wrote down – 100.

Question: Was there a way to untangle all those nice tricks?

Maybe, not 100%, but certainly a better plan. The other declarer won the heart ace at trick one, cashed the heart king, discarding the blocking ace of spades.

He had two chances now, run the spades and hope the spade ten dropped, about a 37% chance, in which case he had nine tricks. If not, he still had a chance the diamonds would come in, about a 50% chance. An overall chance of about 70%.

At this table, North wasn't worried about the percentages. He was busy writing down + 600. Nine tricks: five spades, two hearts, and two diamonds.

UNBLOCKING BUT PLAYING SAFELY

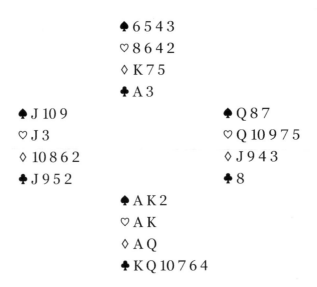

```
                    ♠ 6 5 4 3
                    ♡ 8 6 4 2
                    ◇ K 7 5
                    ♣ A 3
      ♠ J 10 9                      ♠ Q 8 7
      ♡ J 3                         ♡ Q 10 9 7 5
      ◇ 10 8 6 2                    ◇ J 9 4 3
      ♣ J 9 5 2                     ♣ 8
                    ♠ A K 2
                    ♡ A K
                    ◇ A Q
                    ♣ K Q 10 7 6 4
```

Contract: 6 NT

Opening Lead: ♠ Jack

Declarer won the opening lead and cashed the A-Q of diamonds, unblocking the suit. He went to dummy with the club ace and cashed the diamond king, discarding a spade. So far, so good. But when he played a club to his king and East showed out, there was no turning around.

When West won the club jack, he cashed a diamond trick. Down one. "Were you trying to make 7 NT?" asked North, writing -50 with tears in her eyes.

Question: Why was North crying? Was the contract cold despite bad breaks?

The other declarer wanted to insure twelve tricks. After unblocking the diamond A-Q, she played a low club from both hands. When both defenders followed, the contract was safe.

The entry to the diamond king was intact and the long clubs were established. Twelve tricks coming home. "Well done, partner," said North writing + 990.

PART TWO: THE DEFENSE

DEFENSIVE

UNBLOCKING

AND

OPENING LEADS

UNBLOCKING ON DEFENSE

A general principle of unblocking is to avoid being left with a blocking card in partner's suit. A common example:

	A 8 3		When West leads the queen, East must play the king whether declarer plays high or low from dummy.
Q J 10 6 2		K 5	
	9 7 4		

	A 7		West leads the five, dummy plays low, East wins the queen. If East continues the suit, he must return the king, accepting the risk declarer may have the jack.
J 8 6 5 2		K Q 4	
	10 9 3		

	Q 3		West leads the five and the queen wins the trick. East must unblock the jack and hope he can gain the lead.
A 10 7 5 4 2		J 8	
	K 9 6		

	8		West leads the five, East wins the ace and returns the three. When West cashes the K-J, East must be careful to unblock the ten, or he will win the fourth round and the suit is blocked.
K J 7 5 2		A 10 6 3	
	Q 9 4		

BASIC DEFENSIVE UNBLOCKING

Just as a declarer learns to get the short hand's high cards out of the way so the long hand can win the rest of the tricks, the same principle applies in defensive play. Here is a simple basic example.

```
                    ♠ A 4
                    ♡ K 9 5 3
                    ◇ K Q J 7 2
                    ♣ 10 5
     ♠ J 10 9 8 7              ♠ K Q 5
     ♡ 8 2                     ♡ J 10 6 4
     ◇ 6 4 3                   ◇ A 8
     ♣ 8 3 2                   ♣ J 9 6 4
                    ♠ 6 3 2
                    ♡ A Q 7
                    ◇ 10 9 5
                    ♣ A K Q 7
```

Contract: 3 NT
Opening Lead: ♠ Jack

Declarer plays dummy's four. If East plays low, the jack will win and it might seem wasteful to East to play an honor when his partner is going to win the trick. But East must be ready to make a sacrifice for a worthwhile cause. If East plays low, South will make 3 NT.

West will play another spade. When East gets in with his ace of diamonds, he can cash his high spade, but he cannot reach West. South has ten tricks.

Now let's see what happens if East properly "throws away" his queen at trick one. He wins the trick and now must "throw away" his king under the ace in dummy.

But viva la difference! When he wins his diamond ace, he has a low spade to reach West, who cashes the setting tricks. East's careful unblock is a difference of two tricks.

In the coming pages, let's look at a variety of defensive unblocking plays, some more difficult than others.

BASIC DEFENSIVE UNBLOCK

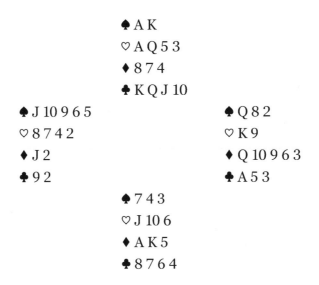

♠ A K
♡ A Q 5 3
♦ 8 7 4
♣ K Q J 10

♠ J 10 9 6 5
♡ 8 7 4 2
♦ J 2
♣ 9 2

♠ Q 8 2
♡ K 9
♦ Q 10 9 6 3
♣ A 5 3

♠ 7 4 3
♡ J 10 6
♦ A K 5
♣ 8 7 6 4

Contract: 3 NT
Opening Lead: ♠ Jack

At trick one, East played an encouraging eight. He knew his partner had at most 2-3 HCP's. At trick two, declarer led the club king. East won and led a low spade knocking out dummy's ace.

Declarer ran the clubs, then came to his hand with the ace of diamonds to take a heart finesse. East won and cashed the spade queen. Declarer had the rest.

Question: Do I even have to ask what went wrong? Bridge 101.

At the other table, when East won the club ace, he returned the spade queen, unblocking the suit. Later he played his small spade to a smiling West.
Down one.

AND BASIC UNBLOCK FROM THE OTHER SIDE

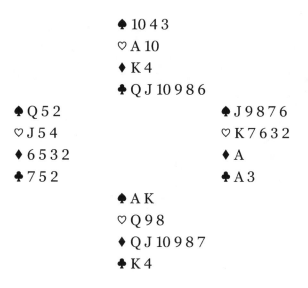

```
              ♠ 10 4 3
              ♡ A 10
              ♦ K 4
              ♣ Q J 10 9 8 6
♠ Q 5 2                        ♠ J 9 8 7 6
♡ J 5 4                        ♡ K 7 6 3 2
♦ 6 5 3 2                      ♦ A
♣ 7 5 2                        ♣ A 3
              ♠ A K
              ♡ Q 9 8
              ♦ Q J 10 9 8 7
              ♣ K 4
```

Contract: 3 NT (N/S bid both minors)
Opening Lead: ♠ 2

East played the six, declarer won the king. Very revealing. Declarer led the club king and East won the ace. He returned the spade seven, declarer won the ace and led a diamond. East took the ace and played a spade. West won the queen.

It's suddenly very quiet. "No more spades?" asked South. "In that case, I have the rest," he said. You could hear East tearing up what was left in his hand.

Question: Sorry, another Bridge 101 hand. What went wrong?

The same thing from the other side. West made a good (lucky?) opening lead, but on the second spade had to unblock the queen. When East won the diamond ace, all his spades were going to cash.

Down one. OK, enough of Bridge 101. Let's get into some others.

UNBLOCKING

ON

OPENING

LEADS

CARDING AGAINST NT: WHEN TO UNBLOCK THE ACE

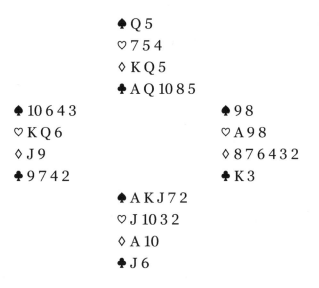

N/S reach 3 NT. West leads the heart king. East plays an encouraging nine. West continues with the heart queen. How should East defend? Unblock and play the ace, or just play the eight?

If West has length, K Q J x (x), better play the ace. If West has K Q x, better not play the ace. South has J x x x and will gain a trick if East plays the ace. How can East tell?

GUIDELINES AND POSSIBILITIES:

K Q x: West leads the king. If encouraged, he continues with the queen. This denies the jack.

K Q J x: West leads the king. If he continues, he should lead the jack next.

K Q J 10 x: Lead the king, then the jack or ten. East will know to overtake with A x x.

Q J x: Lead the queen. If it wins and he judges to continue, lead the jack. This denies the ten.

Q J 10 (x): Lead the queen. If he judges to continue, lead the ten, showing Q J 10, not Q J x.

On the above hand, East should not overtake. The defenders are entitled to three tricks. Declarer is entitled to one trick. By East overtaking, declarer would score two tricks.

NOTRUMP LEADS AND UNBLOCKING PROBLEMS

```
                    ♠ 7 5 2
                    ♡ J 10 8 7
                    ◇ A Q 8
                    ♣ J 5 2
        ♠ K Q J 10              ♠ A 8 3
        ♡ 6 5 4                 ♡ Q 9 3 2
        ◇ 10 9 7 2              ◇ K 6 3
        ♣ 9 4                   ♣ K Q 10
                    ♠ 9 6 4
                    ♡ A K
                    ◇ J 5 4
                    ♣ A 8 7 6 3
```

Contract: 1 NT
Opening Lead: ♠ King

At one table, West continued with the queen. Since that should be shortness, East played low. The suit was blocked. The defenders were entitled to four spades, one diamond, and two clubs. But now they had only three spade tricks.

Question: How could the defenders have untangled their tricks?

The other West, using the guidelines we discussed, led the spade ten at trick two indicating length. East knew to unblock the ace and return the suit. They took their seven tricks. Down one.

Remember, if West shows length, leading first the king, then the jack or ten, he is saying, "Get out of my way."

If he is leading from shortness like K Q x, he is saying, "I'm trying to get out of your way."

MORE NO TRUMP LEADS AND UNBLOCKING PROBLEMS

```
                          ♠ Q 8
                          ♡ A 3
                          ◊ Q 10 8 6 2
                          ♣ A 8 7 4
        ♠ 5                                    ♠ K J 10 9 4 3 2
        ♡ J 7 6 5 2                            ♡ 10 9
        ◊ A 5                                  ◊ 9 7
        ♣ K Q 10 9 5                           ♣ J 6
                          ♠ A 7 6
                          ♡ K Q 8 4
                          ◊ K J 4 3
                          ♣ 3 2
```

North	East	South	West
1 ◊	2 ♠	Dbl	P
3 ♣	P	3 NT	All Pass

Opening Lead: ♣ King

West led the club king, declarer played low, East played the six, declarer played the three. West switched to the spade five. Declarer won and knocked out the diamond ace. Making 3 NT.

West was not happy. "Partner, you had the club jack?" he asked.

Question: What did East do to cause West such grief?

The lead of the king against NT is a power lead, usually from a holding of at least K Q 10 x. The opening leader needs to know the location of the jack in order to know if he should continue. Declarer, with A J x, will almost always hold up, hoping for a continuation (The Bath Coup).

It is not for East to wonder why, just to do or die. Get that jack on the table!

If you don't play it, you don't have it. No questions asked.

A club continuation would have set 3 NT. If East does not have the jack, he should give count. If West wanted partner's attitude, he would lead the ace.

In other words, it's usually Ace=Attitude, King=Kount(sic) or Unblock.

113

DEFENDERS GETTING OUT OF THEIR WAY

UNBLOCKING YOUR SUIT WHILE DEFENDING

♠ K 4
♡ K 8 5
♢ 10 2
♣ A K Q J 10 5

♠ Q 10 5 2   ♠ A 8 7 6 3
♡ A 7 3   ♡ 10 9 4
♢ K 6   ♢ 8 7 5 4
♣ 7 6 4 2   ♣ 3

♠ J 9
♡ Q J 6 2
♢ A Q J 9 3
♣ 9 8

Contract: 3 NT
Opening Lead: ♠ 2

South played low from dummy. East won the ace and returned the six. Declarer won in dummy, playing the nine, then the jack from his hand. West was looking at two spade winners, the heart ace, and the diamond king.

Declarer cashed six club tricks. West followed four times, then had to find two discards. He discarded two small hearts. Declarer led a heart. West won, but after cashing his two spades, had to lead a diamond. South made 3 NT.

Question: How should West have discarded to beat 3 NT?

The other defender gave more thought to the spade situation. South appeared to have started with ♠ J 9 doubleton, so East had five spades. At trick two, West discarded his spade ten, saving the two to unblock the suit.

When West won the heart ace, the defenders had four spade tricks and one heart trick. If declarer had instead finessed in diamonds, he would have gone down an extra trick.

UNBLOCKING ON DEFENSE

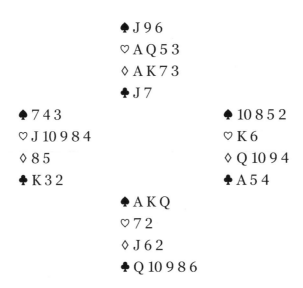

```
                    ♠ J 9 6
                    ♡ A Q 5 3
                    ◇ A K 7 3
                    ♣ J 7
    ♠ 7 4 3                         ♠ 10 8 5 2
    ♡ J 10 9 8 4                    ♡ K 6
    ◇ 8 5                           ◇ Q 10 9 4
    ♣ K 3 2                         ♣ A 5 4
                    ♠ A K Q
                    ♡ 7 2
                    ◇ J 6 2
                    ♣ Q 10 9 8 6
```

Contract: 3 NT
Opening Lead: ♡ Jack

South won the ace at trick one, another heart trick could wait. He led the club jack at trick two. East should have played high, but West won the king and played another heart. Declarer played low, the king fell. East returned a spade.

After another club play, declarer had ten tricks.

Question: Besides the club play, what else could the defenders have done?

At the other table, East unblocked his heart king under the ace at trick one. He won the first club and returned a heart, clearing the suit. When West won the club king, all his hearts were high.

South does best by trying to block the suit, playing low from dummy at trick one, then winning or ducking the second heart.

UNBLOCKING TO GET OUT OF PARTNER'S WAY

                          ♠ 10 3
                          ♡ K Q J 2
                          ◊ J 10 5
                          ♣ 8 6 4 3
        ♠ 9 8 7 4   ♠ K Q J 5 2
        ♡ 9 7 3   ♡ A 8 6
        ◊ 9 8 7 2   ◊ 4
        ♣ 10 9   ♣ K Q 5 2
                          ♠ A 6
                          ♡ 10 5 4
                          ◊ A K Q 6 3
                          ♣ A J 7

South	West	North	East
1 ◊	P	1 ♡	1 ♠
2 NT	P	3 NT	All Pass

Opening Lead: ♠ 9

Declarer played the ten, East the jack, and declarer played the ace. He next led the ten of hearts. West played the three, count, and East won the ace. East led the spade king and everyone followed.

He continued with the queen and was going to run the suit, playing the five next. West won the eight. Making 3 NT.

Question: How should the defenders take five tricks?

West had to get out of the way. At the other table, West played the spade eight and seven when East cashed the king and queen, retaining the four.

When East played the five, it held the trick and East cashed the setting trick, the spade two.

117

UNBLOCKING TO GET OUT OF PARTNER'S WAY

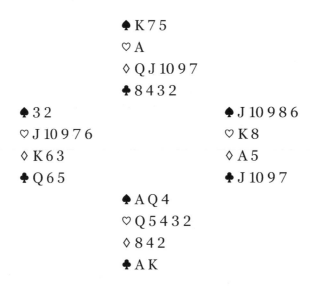

Contract: 3 NT

Opening Lead: ♡ Jack

Declarer's ace won the first trick. He led a diamond from dummy. East properly played high, winning the ace and cashing the heart king. He next led the club jack. Declarer won, knocked out the diamond king and claimed.

Question: At the other table, 3 NT went down. Why?

As you might suspect, East unblocked the heart king under the ace. This gave declarer a second heart trick, but East was getting out of the way. When declarer led a diamond, East made a good play of second hand high. He returned a heart.

Declarer won, but when West won the diamond king, he cashed his heart winners and defeated the contract.

EARLY UNBLOCK AND DIFFICULT SECOND HAND PLAY

                          ♠ K Q 10 4
                          ♡ K 4
                          ◇ J 5 3
                          ♣ A 10 6 5
        ♠ 5 2   ♠ A 7 6 3
        ♡ A Q 9 8 3   ♡ J 2
        ◇ 8 7 2   ◇ 10 9 6 4
        ♣ K 8 2   ♣ 9 7 3
                          ♠ J 9 8
                          ♡ 10 7 6 5
                          ◇ A K Q
                          ♣ Q J 4

South	West	North	East
1 ♣	1 ♡	Dbl	P
1 NT	P	3 NT	All Pass

Opening Lead: ♡ 8

Declarer played the king from dummy, winning the first trick. Then he led the spade four. Let's look at two scenarios:

1) East ducks the spade four. Declarer wins the jack, finesses in clubs and takes nine tricks. Oooooops.
2) East wins the spade ace and returns the heart jack. West can overtake and cash another heart, but that's it. You are finished, toast.

Question: What happened at the other table to defeat 3 NT?

At the other table, play started the same. Declarer won the heart king and led the spade four. Let's look at scenario # 3:

East won the spade ace and having unblocked the heart jack at trick one, returned the heart deuce. Four heart tricks for the good guys. Yea!

Down one.

119

UNBLOCKING TO GET OUT OF PARTNER'S WAY

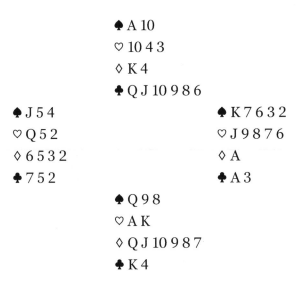

  ♠ A 10
  ♡ 10 4 3
  ◊ K 4
  ♣ Q J 10 9 8 6

♠ J 5 4   ♠ K 7 6 3 2
♡ Q 5 2   ♡ J 9 8 7 6
◊ 6 5 3 2   ◊ A
♣ 7 5 2   ♣ A 3

  ♠ Q 9 8
  ♡ A K
  ◊ Q J 10 9 8 7
  ♣ K 4

South	West	North	East
1 NT	P	3 NT	All Pass

Opening Lead: ♡ 2

Declarer won the first trick with the heart king and started the clubs. East won the second club and returned the heart seven, declarer winning the ace.

Declarer started diamonds. He made 3 NT.

Question: What happened to the above East/West?

West fell asleep with his boring hand and forgot to unblock the heart queen under declarer's ace, as the West player did at the other table.

Of course, if declarer had continued clubs, he might have had a second chance. This resembles a hand in an earlier chapter so no excuses if you blew this one.

A SIMPLE UNBLOCK TO GET OUT OF PARTNER'S WAY

```
                         ♠ A 6 2
                         ♡ 6 3
                         ♢ K Q J 10 9 5
                         ♣ Q 2
        ♠ J 5 4                        ♠ K 9 7
        ♡ J 10 9 8 4                   ♡ Q 2
        ♢ A 3                          ♢ 7 4 2
        ♣ A 8 4                        ♣ 10 9 7 5 3
                         ♠ Q 10 8 3
                         ♡ A K 7 5
                         ♢ 8 6
                         ♣ K J 6
```

Contract: 3 NT
Opening Lead: ♡ Jack

South won the opening lead and played diamonds. When West took the ace and continued hearts, what did East do?

It depends what he did at trick one. If he still had the heart queen, declarer would duck. East would have to start another suit. Declarer would start the clubs, still having a heart stopper.

Ten tricks. One spade, two hearts, five diamonds, and two clubs.

Question: How should the defense proceed to defeat 3 NT?

At the other table, East unblocked the heart queen at trick one. Now declarer could not hold up. West would win the race, being able to set up and cash five tricks before declarer could score nine.

DIFFICULT UNBLOCK KNOWING IT WILL COST A TRICK

```
                        ♠ Q 6 3 2
                        ♡ Q 4 3
                        ◊ J 4
                        ♣ A K 7 4
        ♠ 8 5 4                         ♠ J 10 9 7
        ♡ J 10 9 7 5                    ♡ K 6
        ◊ A K 5                         ◊ 7 6 2
        ♣ 9 8                           ♣ Q J 10 6
                        ♠ A K
                        ♡ A 8 2
                        ◊ Q 10 9 8 3
                        ♣ 5 3 2
```

Contract: 3 NT
Opening Lead: ♡ Jack

East/West had the agreement that leading the jack denied a higher honor. From ♡ A J 10 x x, the lead would be the ten. Declarer played low. East knew declarer had the ace and with the queen in dummy, he didn't want to throw the king under the bus.

Declarer won the ace and started the diamonds. West won and continued hearts. Declarer ducked and East won. East had to play another suit.

Declarer forced out the other high diamond and had the rest. Ten tricks.

Question: How would the defense do if East threw the king under the bus?

A lot better. Declarer can win or duck, but West will win the first diamond and give declarer his other high heart. But West will win the race for home.

Final score: E/W 5 tricks, N/S 8 tricks.   E/W win.

WINNING HIGH TO UNBLOCK

```
                    ♠ 10 7 3
                    ♡ K 9 4
                    ◊ K J 8
                    ♣ Q J 10 7
   ♠ Q 8 4                          ♠ 9 6 5 2
   ♡ Q 10 8 7 3                     ♡ A J
   ◊ A 6 3                          ◊ 7 5 2
   ♣ 6 2                            ♣ 8 5 4 3
                    ♠ A K J
                    ♡ 6 5 2
                    ◊ Q 10 9 4
                    ♣ A K 9
```

Contract: 3 NT
Opening Lead: ♡ 7

Declarer played low. Using the Rule of Eleven, East knew if he played the jack it would win. He also remembered being told something about keeping honor cards over dummy's honor cards. So he played the jack.

Whether he continued or switched, declarer had nine tricks after knocking out the diamond ace. The heart suit was blocked.
Four clubs, three diamonds, and two spades.

Question: Did East overthink at trick one and miss the bigger picture?

Yup. Rule of Eleven, keeping honors, all that is good, but unblocking is king!
If East just wins the heart ace and returns the jack, West will overtake with the queen and force out the king.

When West wins the diamond ace, declarer is down one. He loses four hearts and one diamond.

UNBLOCKING TO GET OUT OF THE WAY

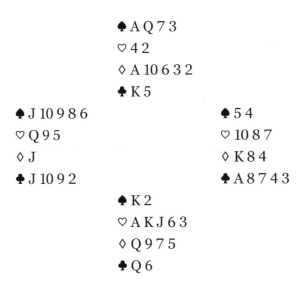

```
                        ♠ A Q 7 3
                        ♡ 4 2
                        ♢ A 10 6 3 2
                        ♣ K 5
        ♠ J 10 9 8 6              ♠ 5 4
        ♡ Q 9 5                   ♡ 10 8 7
        ♢ J                       ♢ K 8 4
        ♣ J 10 9 2                ♣ A 8 7 4 3
                        ♠ K 2
                        ♡ A K J 6 3
                        ♢ Q 9 7 5
                        ♣ Q 6
```

Contract: 3 NT

Opening Lead: ???

At one table, West led the spade jack. Declarer made 3 NT. When comparing with her teammates, she asked, "What did you lead on this board?"

"I led the club jack," replied West. "Very nice," she said. "So you beat 3 NT?"

Question: Did the other West defeat 3 NT?

Well, it depended on what he played when East won the club ace and returned the suit. Did you unblock the nine or ten?

If you did, E/W scored four club tricks and one red trick. If not, the club suit was blocked.

Don't tell anyone if you did that.

MORE "GET OUT OF MY WAY"

```
                        ♠ Q J
                        ♡ K J 7 3
                        ◇ Q 8 3
                        ♣ J 7 6 3
        ♠ 10 5 2                       ♠ A K 9 6 4
        ♡ A 9 5 2                      ♡ 8 6 4
        ◇ 10 9 4                       ◇ 6 2
        ♣ 8 5 2                        ♣ 10 9 4
                        ♠ 8 7 3
                        ♡ Q 10
                        ◇ A K J 7 5
                        ♣ A K Q
```

South	West	North	East
1 ◇	P	1 ♡	P
2 NT	P	3 NT	All Pass

Opening Lead: ♠ 2

East won the opening lead with the king. He continued with the spade ace and another spade. West won the spade ten. He could do no more than cash the heart ace. Declarer had the rest. Nine tricks for the bad guys.

Question: How could West have known to unblock the spade ten?

Mike Lawrence wrote a great article ("ACBL Bulletin," February, 2021) discussing how to handle this difficult situation.

Instead of winning the first trick with the spade king, Mike suggested to win the ace, then cash the king. This unusual sequence of plays should convey an unusual message, in this case being "Get out of my way."

If West unblocked the spade ten at trick two, the defense would cash five spade tricks and the heart ace. Down two.

A similar layout could be:

```
                                ♡ 8 2
        ♡ Q 6 5                         ♡ A K J 7 4
                        ♡ 10 9 3
```

DIFFICULT UNBLOCK OF YOUR OWN SUIT

♠ 8 6 4 3
♡ A 10
◇ Q J 4
♣ A Q 10 8

♠ A 10 2
♡ Q 6 5
◇ 10 9 8 7
♣ 6 5 4

♠ K 9 7 5
♡ 8 3 2
◇ 5 3
♣ K J 9 3

♠ Q J
♡ K J 9 7 4
◇ A K 6 2
♣ 7 2

Contract: 3 NT
Opening Lead: ◇ 10

Declarer won the opening lead in dummy, cashed the heart ace, and took a heart finesse. West counted declarer for nine tricks, so he switched to spades, leading the spade two. He won the third spade, but the suit was blocked. Declarer had nine tricks.

If he had led the spade ace, then the ten, West could not afford to overtake. Dummy's eight would soon be high.

Question: How could the defense have prevailed? The spade switch was right.

The West at the other table started the spades by leading the ten. East won the king, over to West's ace, then the spade two thru dummy's ♠ 8 6, East's ♠ 9 7.

On opening lead, it's the same problem if you choose to lead this suit. Start with a difficult-to-read ten to avoid blocking the suit.

UNBLOCKING PARTNER'S SUIT

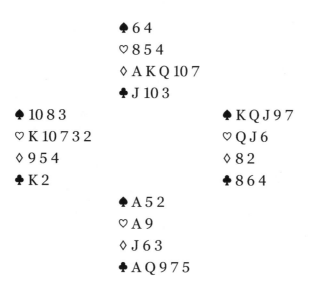

```
                    ♠ 6 4
                    ♡ 8 5 4
                    ◊ A K Q 10 7
                    ♣ J 10 3
    ♠ 10 8 3                        ♠ K Q J 9 7
    ♡ K 10 7 3 2                    ♡ Q J 6
    ◊ 9 5 4                         ◊ 8 2
    ♣ K 2                           ♣ 8 6 4
                    ♠ A 5 2
                    ♡ A 9
                    ◊ J 6 3
                    ♣ A Q 9 7 5
```

Contract: 3 NT

Opening Lead: ♡ 3

East played the jack and declarer won, perhaps fearful of a spade switch. He crossed to dummy with a high diamond to take a club finesse. West won and played the heart king, everyone followed. When West played another heart, East won the queen. Declarer had the rest. The yelling started.

"Why didn't you play a low heart first?" yelled East. Remember, he who yells first is usually the one who is wrong. "Why didn't you unblock the queen under the king? " replied West. "I was afraid you might now have a singleton queen."

Question: Who shall we blame for this terrible result?

All East's fault. Yes, he might have started with ♡ Q J doubleton, and by leading low, West would have blocked the suit. The lead of the king was fine.

East just had to get out of the way.

DOUBLE UNBLOCK

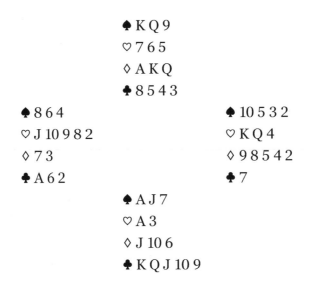

♠ K Q 9
♡ 7 6 5
◇ A K Q
♣ 8 5 4 3

♠ 8 6 4
♡ J 10 9 8 2
◇ 7 3
♣ A 6 2

♠ 10 5 3 2
♡ K Q 4
◇ 9 8 5 4 2
♣ 7

♠ A J 7
♡ A 3
◇ J 10 6
♣ K Q J 10 9

Contract: 3 NT
Opening Lead: ♡ Jack

The first trick went five, four, three. West continued another heart, declarer won the ace and led a club, West won the ace and continued hearts. East won, but declarer had the rest.

"Can't you ever get out of my way?" moaned West.

Question: How should East have carded to defeat the contract?

At the other table, East unblocked his heart suit twice, playing the queen at his first opportunity, then the king. When West won the club ace, the heart suit was ready to run.

The defenders took four hearts and one club.

BE CAREFUL NOT TO BLOCK YOUR OWN SUIT

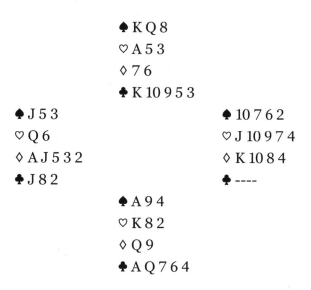

Contract: 3 NT

Opening Lead: ◊ 3

East won the first trick with the king and returned the diamond four. West captured the queen with his ace and cashed the jack. It didn't matter which diamond East played, the suit was blocked. Declarer took the next nine tricks.

"Partner, can't you please pay attention to the spot cards?" begged East.

Question: Could you have correctly read the spot cards and done the right thing?

At the other table, West thought about the diamond four. Could East have started with only two diamonds? The four was clearly his lowest. Then declarer would have had ◊ Q 10 9 8 and would not have played the queen.

No, it was more logical that East had four diamonds. So instead of cashing, he returned a low diamond. The defense took five diamond tricks.

UNBLOCKING TO GET OUT OF THE WAY – NOT ALWAYS

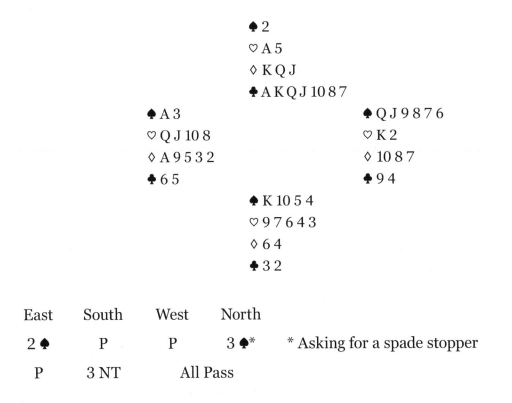

East	South	West	North	
2 ♠	P	P	3 ♣*	* Asking for a spade stopper
P	3 NT	All Pass		

Opening Lead: ♡ Queen

Declarer played the ace and East, having just read this book, unblocked the king. After cashing seven club tricks, declarer played a diamond. West could only take four tricks. Making 3 NT.

Question: How did the defense defeat 3 NT at the other table?

Well, there is a time and place for everything, and always an exception to the rule. East needed his partner to have the spade and diamond aces or South had nine tricks. If so, nothing was blocked. West could cross to East's heart king and East could cross back to West.

East held on to his heart king. When West won the diamond ace, he led low to East's king of hearts. East switched to the spade queen. The defense took two spades, three hearts, and one diamond. Down two.

DEFENDER UNBLOCKS HIS ACE

                        ♠ J 3
                        ♡ A 10 3
                        ◊ 10 8
                        ♣ K J 10 7 6 3
        ♠ 4   ♠ Q 10 9 8 7
        ♡ K 4 2   ♡ 9 8 6 5
        ◊ J 9 7 6 4 2   ◊ A Q
        ♣ A 5 4   ♣ 8 2
                        ♠ A K 6 5 2
                        ♡ Q J 7
                        ◊ K 5 3
                        ♣ Q 9

Contract: 3 NT

Opening Lead: ◊ 6

East won the ace and returned the queen. Declarer ducked and East switched to a low spade. Declarer won and after forcing out the club ace, he took a heart finesse for ten tricks.

Question: How did the defense prevail at the other table?

The other East, familiar with the normal defensive play of the queen from A Q x, played the queen from her A-Q at trick one. What could declarer do? Afraid to hold up if West had led from ◊ A J 7 6 4 2, he won the king at trick one.

When he started the clubs, West held up until the third round, allowing East to unblock the diamond ace.
West won the third club and cashed five diamond tricks.

DIFFICULT UNBLOCKING

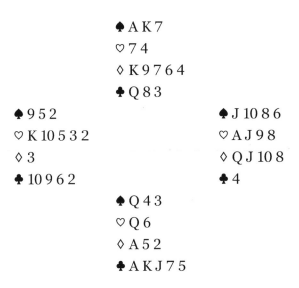

```
                    ♠ A K 7
                    ♡ 7 4
                    ◇ K 9 7 6 4
                    ♣ Q 8 3
       ♠ 9 5 2                        ♠ J 10 8 6
       ♡ K 10 5 3 2                   ♡ A J 9 8
       ◇ 3                            ◇ Q J 10 8
       ♣ 10 9 6 2                     ♣ 4
                    ♠ Q 4 3
                    ♡ Q 6
                    ◇ A 5 2
                    ♣ A K J 7 5
```

Contract: 3 NT
Opening Lead: ♡ 3

East won the first trick with the ace and returned the jack. West captured the queen with his king. Believing declarer started with ♡ Q 9 6, and afraid to return a low heart, West cashed the ten. East won the fourth heart, but the suit was now blocked. The defense took four heart tricks, and declarer took the rest.

Question: What was the cause of this major car crash?

Not as easy as it looks. Yes, if East returns the heart eight at trick two, and West doesn't cash the ten at trick three, but instead plays low, everything is fine. Then the heart nine to the ten for five tricks.

At the other table, East returned the heart eight, his original fourth best, or low from three, or he started with only two, in which case 3 NT was unbeatable.

West won the king and did return a low heart to East. After East cashed the jack, he played his last heart, the nine, to West's ♥ 10 2 for the setting tricks.

DIFFICULT DEFENSIVE UNBLOCK

```
                        ♠ A 9 8 7
                        ♡ K J 7
                        ♢ 4
                        ♣ A 8 5 3 2
        ♠ K J 10                        ♠ 5 3 2
        ♡ 10 5                          ♡ A 9 8 3
        ♢ Q 8 5 3 2                     ♢ K J 9 6
        ♣ 10 7 6                        ♣ J 9
                        ♠ Q 6 4
                        ♡ Q 6 4 2
                        ♢ A 10 7
                        ♣ K Q 4
```

South	West	North	East
1 ♣	P	1 ♠	P
1 NT	P	3 NT	All Pass

Opening Lead: ♢ 3

East won the first trick with the diamond king and returned the diamond six, low from ♢ J 9 6. Declarer ducked and West won the queen. West was sure declarer remained with the singleton ace and wanted to clear the diamond suit with a high suit preference eight, but already could see the problem.

He returned the five, declarer won the ace. When declarer finished running the clubs, he played a heart. East won the ace, but the diamond suit was blocked. East had the singleton nine, West had the eight and the deuce. Making 3 NT.

Question: How could the defenders have untangled the diamonds?

Not easily. At the other table, East was pretty sure West had started with five diamonds, both from the bidding and the early play. In anticipation of the problem, he returned the diamond jack at trick two. The nine would have worked too, as long as he kept the six.

The defense took four diamonds and one heart, down one.

GETTING OUT OF PARTNER'S WAY

♠ A Q 4
♡ 6 5 4 2
◇ Q J 10
♣ K 8 7

♠ 10 8 2   ♠ J 9 6 5
♡ 10 9 8 7   ♡ K Q J
◇ A 6 5 3   ◇ 2
♣ 5 4   ♣ A 10 9 3 2

♠ K 7 3
♡ A 3
◇ K 9 8 7 4
♣ Q J 6

South	West	North	East
1 ◇	P	1 ♡	P
1 NT	P	3 NT	All Pass

Opening Lead: ♡ 10

West led the heart ten, dummy's bid suit. East won the jack. He continued with the heart king and declarer won the ace. Declarer led a low diamond towards dummy's queen, then played another diamond. West won the ace and played a heart. East won and had only one more defensive trick, the club ace.

"Partner, I made the winning lead, can't you help out?" pleaded West.

Question: What help was West referring to? What could East do to set 3 NT?

At the other table, West led the heart ten. The defense started the same, but on the second diamond, East discarded the heart king, unblocking the suit.

When West won the diamond ace, she cashed two heart tricks. The defenders took three heart tricks and two aces. Down one.

DEFENDERS UNBLOCK TO TAKE ALL THEIR TRICKS

```
                    ♠ A J 10 3
                    ♡ J 7
                    ◊ 8 6 3
                    ♣ Q J 5 4
        ♠ 9 2                       ♠ K 8 5 4
        ♡ Q 10 6 4                  ♡ K 9 5 3 2
        ◊ K 9 7 5                   ◊ J 10
        ♣ K 6 3                     ♣ 8 2
                    ♠ Q 7 6
                    ♡ A 8
                    ◊ A Q 4 2
                    ♣ A 10 9 7
```

South	West	North	East
1 NT	P	2 ♣	P
2 ◊	P	2 NT	All Pass

Opening Lead: ♡ 4

Declarer played the jack, East won the king and returned the three. Declarer won and led the spade queen. East won the king and returned the two of hearts. West won the ten and cashed the queen.

East is still sitting there with the good heart. Declarer took eight tricks: three spades, one heart, three clubs, and one diamond. Making 2 NT.

Question: How should the defenders untangle their tricks?

At the other table, West unblocked the ten (or queen) under declarer's ace of hearts, keeping the four. When he was in with one of his minor kings, he had the heart four to reach East.

Down one.

UNBLOCKING FOR PARTNER

```
                      ♠ K 7 6 3
                      ♡ Q J 4 2
                      ◇ A
                      ♣ Q 8 6 2
         ♠ 10 8                        ♠ Q J 9 2
         ♡ 9 7 3                       ♡ 10 8 6 5
         ◇ K 9 7 6 2                   ◇ Q J 8
         ♣ K 7 3                       ♣ 5 4
                      ♠ A 5 4
                      ♡ A K
                      ◇ 10 5 4 3
                      ♣ A J 10 9
```

Contract: 3 NT

Opening Lead: ◇ 6

Declarer won the ace in dummy and led a club. West won and returned a diamond. East cashed the ◇ Q J. However, with no way to reach West, declarer had the rest. West was very forlorn, writing - 600.

Question: I'm sure you are getting tired of this question by now, but?

At the other table, East played the queen at trick one. Some might play the jack but that should deny the queen and suggest the ten.

If you unblocked the queen and then played the jack, + 100.

UNBLOCKING TO TAKE ALL YOUR TRICKS

```
                        ♠ Q 9 8 7 5 4
                        ♡ J 8 7
                        ◊ K J
                        ♣ J 7
      ♠ J 2                              ♠ A K 10 3
      ♡ K 6 4 3                          ♡ A 9 2
      ◊ 6 5 3                            ◊ 9 4 2
      ♣ 9 5 4 2                          ♣ 10 8 3
                        ♠ 6
                        ♡ Q 10 5
                        ◊ A Q 10 8 7
                        ♣ A K Q 5
```

South	West	North	East
1 ◊	P	1 ♠	P
2 ♣	P	2 ♠	P
2 NT	P	3 NT	All Pass

Opening Lead: ♡ 3

East won the heart ace at trick one. South's most likely distribution was 1-3-4-5. East cashed the spade king, then returned the heart nine. West won the king. He played the spade jack. Declarer ducked and had nine tricks. Three clubs, five diamonds, and one heart.

"Didn't you read Dr J's book?" asked East.

Question: How should West have defended?

At the other table, West unblocked the spade jack when East played the king. Now when West won the heart king, he could lead the spade two and declarer could not duck. The defense took two hearts and three spades. Down one.

UNBLOCKING PARTNER'S SUIT

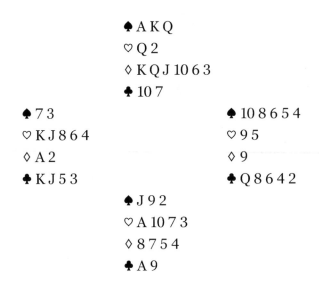

♠ A K Q
♡ Q 2
◇ K Q J 10 6 3
♣ 10 7

♠ 7 3
♡ K J 8 6 4
◇ A 2
♣ K J 5 3

♠ 10 8 6 5 4
♡ 9 5
◇ 9
♣ Q 8 6 4 2

♠ J 9 2
♡ A 10 7 3
◇ 8 7 5 4
♣ A 9

West	North	East	South
1 ♡	2 ♦	P	3 ♦
P	3 ♡	P	3 NT
	All Pass		

Opening Lead: ♣ 3

West was warned off a heart lead by East's pass over North's 3 ♡ bid. East would have doubled if he had a heart honor. East played the club queen and declarer ducked. East continued with the club four. Declarer won the ace and started the diamonds.

West won and cashed the ♣ K J, but the suit was blocked. Making 3 NT.

Question: After finding such a good opening lead, what went wrong?

At the other table, West made the same opening lead. But when declarer won the club ace, West unblocked a club honor. When he won the diamond ace, he cashed one high club and had a low one to reach East. Down one.

AVOIDING

THE

ENDPLAY

BY UNBLOCKING

DEFENDER TRIES TO AVOID THE ENDPLAY

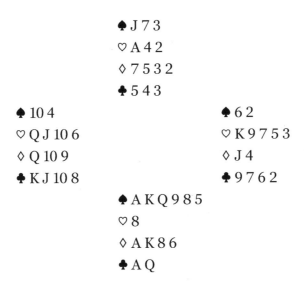

```
                    ♠ J 7 3
                    ♡ A 4 2
                    ◊ 7 5 3 2
                    ♣ 5 4 3
   ♠ 10 4                        ♠ 6 2
   ♡ Q J 10 6                    ♡ K 9 7 5 3
   ◊ Q 10 9                      ◊ J 4
   ♣ K J 10 8                    ♣ 9 7 6 2
                    ♠ A K Q 9 8 5
                    ♡ 8
                    ◊ A K 8 6
                    ♣ A Q
```

Contract: 6 ♠

Opening Lead: ♡ Queen

Declarer won the opening lead and drew trumps. She tried a club finesse. West won the king and led another heart. At least diamonds were 3-2. Down only one.

Question: Unavoidable or was there a better plan?

The declarer at the other table tried something different. He won the opening heart lead and ruffed a heart high. He led a trump to the jack and then another heart ruff.

After drawing the last trumps, when they divided 2-2, he cashed the A-K of diamonds and played a third diamond.

West tried to avoid the endplay by unblocking the queen, then the ten of diamonds under the A-K, but he was forced to win the third diamond with the nine and lead a club from his king. Right idea, good try.

FINESSE ? PARTIAL ELIMINATION & UNBLOCK

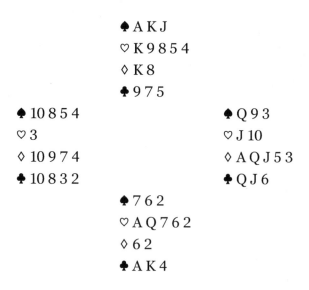

♠ A K J
♡ K 9 8 5 4
◊ K 8
♣ 9 7 5

♠ 10 8 5 4
♡ 3
◊ 10 9 7 4
♣ 10 8 3 2

♠ Q 9 3
♡ J 10
◊ A Q J 5 3
♣ Q J 6

♠ 7 6 2
♡ A Q 7 6 2
◊ 6 2
♣ A K 4

Contract: 4 ♡
Opening Lead: ◊ 10

East won the first two tricks and switched to a trump. Declarer drew trumps and trying to avoid the spade finesse, cashed the A-K of clubs and another club.

West shifted to a spade. Down one.

Question: How did the other declarer make four hearts?

Play was the same for the first three tricks. Before drawing the last trump, declarer cashed the A-K of clubs. Why? To try to endplay East, if possible, to play a spade.

Did you notice at the first table West switched to a spade? How did West get on lead after A-K of clubs and a club? Because East defended well. He could see the endplay coming now, and unblocked the Q-J of clubs under the A-K.

Do you think it would be as easy, if before drawing all the trumps, for East to see he must play the club queen under the ace? And the jack under the king?

A good declarer will make this play as early in the hand as possible, not at the end when everyone knows what is happening. Try to catch a defender napping.

UNBLOCKING TO AVOID THE ENDPLAY

$$\spadesuit\ K\ Q\ J$$
$$\heartsuit\ 10\ 4\ 2$$
$$\diamond\ 9\ 6\ 3$$
$$\clubsuit\ 8\ 7\ 5\ 2$$

$$\spadesuit\ A\ 6 \qquad\qquad \spadesuit\ 10\ 5\ 3\ 2$$
$$\heartsuit\ K\ 7\ 5 \qquad\qquad \heartsuit\ J\ 9\ 8\ 6$$
$$\diamond\ Q\ J\ 4 \qquad\qquad \diamond\ 10\ 8\ 7\ 5$$
$$\clubsuit\ K\ Q\ J\ 9\ 3 \qquad\qquad \clubsuit\ 6$$

$$\spadesuit\ 9\ 8\ 7\ 4$$
$$\heartsuit\ A\ Q\ 3$$
$$\diamond\ A\ K\ 2$$
$$\clubsuit\ A\ 7\ 5$$

West	North	East	South
1 ♣	P	1 ◊	1 NT
	All Pass		

Opening Lead: ♣ King

Declarer won the opening lead and led a spade. West won, cashed his clubs, and exited a spade. Declarer cashed the A-K of diamonds and led a small diamond. West was endplayed. He led a heart. Declarer took seven tricks.

Question: How did the defenders defeat 1 NT at the other table?

West was not sleeping. He unblocked the ◊ Q-J under the ◊ A-K. East won the third diamond and played a heart.

Of course, every time I make that play, declarer started with ◊ A K 10 .

UNBLOCKING TO AVOID BEING ENDPLAYED

```
                    ♠ Q J 9 8
                    ♡ J 9 6 4
                    ◇ 8 3
                    ♣ A K 2
        ♠ 7 3                           ♠ 5 4
        ♡ K 7                           ♡ Q 10 8 3
        ◇ Q 7 5 2                       ◇ J 10 6 4
        ♣ Q J 10 6 4                    ♣ 8 7 5
                    ♠ A K 10 6 2
                    ♡ A 5 2
                    ◇ A K 9
                    ♣ 9 3
```

Contract: 6 ♠

Opening Lead: ♣ Queen

Declarer won the opening lead and cashed the heart ace. He drew trumps, then played the A-K of diamonds and ruffed a diamond. He cashed the club king and ruffed a club. Then came a low heart towards dummy. West won the king.

Making six spades. The ruff/sluff allowed declarer to dispose of a heart loser.

Question: East asked West, "Why did you still have the heart king?"

Good question. Declarer made a good play by cashing the heart ace early. If he had eliminated all the side suits first, probably my tailor could have seen what was happening and unblocked the heart king.

But if declarer had the ten or queen of hearts, why is he cashing the ace, a defender should be asking himself? Doesn't declarer know how to take a finesse?

UNBLOCKING TO CREATE AN ENTRY FOR PARTNER

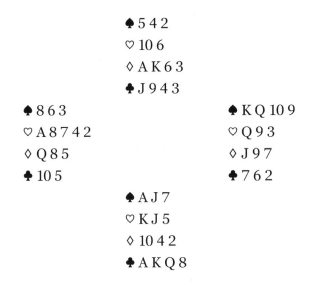

♠ 5 4 2
♡ 10 6
◇ A K 6 3
♣ J 9 4 3

♠ 8 6 3
♡ A 8 7 4 2
◇ Q 8 5
♣ 10 5

♠ K Q 10 9
♡ Q 9 3
◇ J 9 7
♣ 7 6 2

♠ A J 7
♡ K J 5
◇ 10 4 2
♣ A K Q 8

Contract: 3 NT
Opening Lead: ♡ 4

East played the nine at trick one and declarer won the jack. With eight tricks, declarer had to keep East, the danger hand, off lead. Diamonds seemed the best source for a ninth trick, either 3-3 or doubleton Q-J.

When declarer led a diamond, West played the queen, a good play. Declarer won and diamonds were 3-3. But now East, the danger hand, won the third diamond and returned the heart queen. Down one.

Question: Was there any hope for this contract after West's good play?

At the other table, play went the same way except when West played the diamond queen trying to unblock, declarer countered by ducking. The defense was helpless. Declarer won the return. Since diamonds were 3-3, declarer had nine tricks.

UNBLOCKING TO AVOID THE ENDPLAY

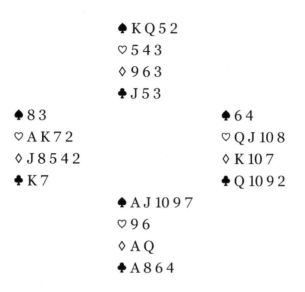

```
                    ♠ K Q 5 2
                    ♡ 5 4 3
                    ◊ 9 6 3
                    ♣ J 5 3
        ♠ 8 3                       ♠ 6 4
        ♡ A K 7 2                   ♡ Q J 10 8
        ◊ J 8 5 4 2                 ◊ K 10 7
        ♣ K 7                       ♣ Q 10 9 2
                    ♠ A J 10 9 7
                    ♡ 9 6
                    ◊ A Q
                    ♣ A 8 6 4
```

Contract: 4 ♠

Opening Lead: ♡ Ace

West led the heart ace, East played the queen, and West continued with a low heart. East won and persisted with another heart (not best). South ruffed, cashed the club ace and led a trump to dummy.

After a successful diamond finesse, declarer cashed the diamond ace, led a trump to dummy and ruffed the last diamond.

Declarer led a club. West won and was endplayed. When he led a red card, the ruff/ sluff gave declarer the contract.

Question: Assess the blame. East, West, or both?

Both. West was sleeping at trick four. Why is declarer cashing the club ace? If he had the queen, wouldn't he probably take a finesse? If West unblocks his club king under the ace, he avoids the endplay.

But East should have shifted to clubs at trick three. Why was West putting him in? If another heart was best, West would have done that himself.

UNBLOCKING A TRUMP TO AVOID AN ENDPLAY

```
                    ♠ A 10 6 4 2
                    ♡ Q J 9
                    ◊ 10 8 4
                    ♣ K 7
        ♠ Q                        ♠ K 7
        ♡ 10 8 3                   ♡ K 7 4
        ◊ A K J 9 6 2              ◊ 7 3
        ♣ 10 4 3                   ♣ J 9 8 6 5 2
                    ♠ J 9 8 5 3
                    ♡ A 6 5 2
                    ◊ Q 5
                    ♣ A Q
```

South	West	North	East
1 ♠	3 ◊	4 ♠	All Pass

Opening Lead: ◊ Ace

West led the A-K of diamonds, then the jack ruffed by South. Declarer led a spade to the ace. He cashed the A-K of clubs and played a spade. East was endplayed.

Left to his own devices, declarer had a slow heart loser. After the ruff/sluff, then one heart finesse was sufficient. Making four spades.

Question: How did the defenders defeat four spades in the other room?

East could see it coming. He unblocked by ruffing the third round of diamonds with the spade king and exiting a trump. The defenders sat back and waited for their heart trick. If South had the heart ten, there was no defense anyhow.

UNBLOCKING A TRUMP TO AVOID AN ENDPLAY

```
                    ♠ 10 9 7 6 3
                    ♡ K 8 6 4 3
                    ◇ K 5
                    ♣ K
        ♠ 4                         ♠ A Q J 2
        ♡ A 10                      ♡ Q
        ◇ J 10 9 4                  ◇ 8 7 6 3 2
        ♣ 9 7 6 5 3 2               ♣ 10 8 4
                    ♠ K 8 5
                    ♡ J 9 7 5 2
                    ◇ A Q
                    ♣ A Q J
```

South	West	North	East
1 NT	P	2◇*	P	* Transfer
3 ♡	P	4 ♡	All Pass

Opening Lead: ♠ 4

East won the opening lead and returned the spade queen. West ruffed declarer's king and led the diamond jack. Declarer cashed all his minor winners and played a trump. West was endplayed. The ruff/sluff allowed declarer to avoid a spade loser. Making four hearts.

Question: How did the defenders defeat four hearts at the other table?

Frank Stewart commented on this hand from the ACBL Summer Nationals in 2019, when the Daily Bulletin extolled South's play. Frank noted South's play was routine; it was West who erred by not unblocking the trump ace at trick three.

The bidding clearly marked declarer with the minor aces. West avoids the endplay and four hearts is down one, having an unavoidable late spade loser.

ANOTHER UNBLOCK TO AVOID THE ENDPLAY

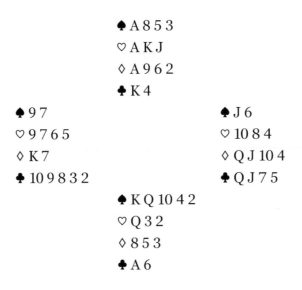

Contract: 6 ♠

Opening Lead: ♣ 10

Declarer won the opening lead in hand, played a diamond to the ace and drew trumps. She cashed three high hearts and the club king. Then she led a diamond. West won and was endplayed. The resultant ruff/sluff avoided a second diamond loser. Making six spades.

"Could you try paying attention?" asked East, writing -1430.

Question: What was East referring to?

At the other table, West was paying attention. And he had bought a copy of this book. When declarer cashed the diamond ace at trick two, West thought, "That's a very strange play. He can't have the queen." So he threw his king under the ace.

East won the second diamond trick and cashed the setting trick. "Nice play," East said to West as he wrote +100.

A DIFFICULT UNBLOCK TO AVOID THE ENDPLAY

                              ♠ 10 8 3
                              ♡ Q 9 2
                              ◊ A 4 3
                              ♣ Q 7 6 2
        ♠ A Q 9 4   ♠ J 7 6 2
        ♡ 8 6   ♡ 7 5 4
        ◊ K Q 10 9 5   ◊ J 8 7
        ♣ K 10   ♣ J 4 3
                              ♠ K 5
                              ♡ A K J 10 3
                              ◊ 6 2
                              ♣ A 9 8 5

Contract: 4 ♡

Opening Lead: ◊ King

Declarer ducked the opening lead and won the diamond continuation. He led a low club to his ace and cashed the A-Q of trumps. He ruffed dummy's last diamond and led a club. West was endplayed.

His choices were to cash the spade ace or offer a ruff/sluff. Either way, declarer would lose only three tricks.

Question: How can West avoid the endplay?

West had to unblock the club king under the ace, creating an entry in East's hand to lead a spade later. If declarer had ♣ A J, why was he cashing the ace?

AVOIDING THE ENDPLAY

```
                        ♠ A
                        ♡ 10 9 6 4
                        ◇ K 9 4 2
                        ♣ A K Q 9
        ♠ Q 9 5 4                      ♠ J 10 8 7
        ♡ A J 8 2                      ♡ Q 5 3
        ◇ A Q                          ◇ J 10 5
        ♣ J 7 5                        ♣ 8 6 4
                        ♠ K 6 3 2
                        ♡ K 7
                        ◇ 8 7 6 3
                        ♣ 10 3 2
```

North	East	South	West
1 ◇	P	1 ♠	P
2 ♡	P	2 NT	P
3 NT		All Pass	

Opening Lead: ♣ 5

Declarer won the opening lead in hand and led a diamond. West played the ace and shifted to a spade. Declarer cashed three club tricks and led the diamond king, dropping West's queen.

He played another diamond. East won the jack and played the spade jack. Declarer won the king. West, reduced to ♠ Q 9 ♡ A J 8, played the spade nine.

Declarer led a spade, endplaying West. Declarer's heart king was his ninth trick.

Question: How did West defend at the other table?

Too easy a question, by now. Obviously, West unblocked the spade queen under the king, playing East for the spade ten along with the jack. When East won the next spade, the heart lead thru declarer's king meant down one.

150

DIFFICULT UNBLOCKING IN TRUMPS

♠ 7 6 3
♡ Q J 10 7
◇ 9
♣ 6 5 4 3 2

♠ K Q 10 8 4 2
♡ 2
◇ 3 2
♣ Q J 10 8

♠ J
♡ K 5
◇ K Q J 10 8 7 6 5 4
♣ 9

♠ A 9 5
♡ A 9 8 6 4 3
◇ A
♣ A K 7

East	South	West	North
5 ◇	5 ♡	All Pass	

Opening Lead: ♠ King

Declarer won the ace and played the heart ace. He cashed the ace of diamonds, then A-K of clubs. East ruffed the second club. If East didn't ruff, declarer was going to play a trump next.

Reduced to only diamonds, he led a high diamond, giving declarer a sluff/sluff, discarding a losing club from hand, a spade from dummy. Still on lead, another diamond gave declarer a ruff/sluff, making five hearts.

Question: How did the defenders defeat five hearts at the other table?

When declarer led the trump ace, East unblocked the trump king. Declarer lost no trump tricks, but now lost two spades and a club to West.

YOU ARE NOT GOING TO ENDPLAY ME

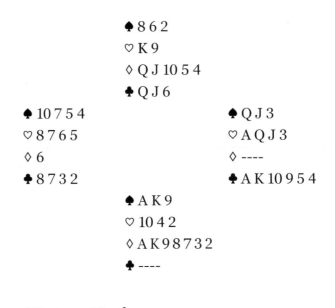

```
                    ♠ 8 6 2
                    ♡ K 9
                    ◊ Q J 10 5 4
                    ♣ Q J 6
   ♠ 10 7 5 4                        ♠ Q J 3
   ♡ 8 7 6 5                         ♡ A Q J 3
   ◊ 6                               ◊ ----
   ♣ 8 7 3 2                         ♣ A K 10 9 5 4
                    ♠ A K 9
                    ♡ 10 4 2
                    ◊ A K 9 8 7 3 2
                    ♣ ----
```

East	South	West	North
1 ♣	1 ◊	P	2 ♣
Dbl	5 ◊	All Pass	

Opening Lead: ♣ 2

Declare played the jack from dummy, East covered and declarer ruffed. He cashed the A-K of spades and led a diamond to dummy. He ruffed a club and went to dummy again with a trump. After ruffing the last club, declarer led a spade.

East was endplayed. Declarer lost only one spade and one heart.

Question: How did declarer go down at the other table? Poor technique?

No, better defense. East was not sleeping. Having been unlucky to have not received a heart lead, he could see the endplay coming. When South cashed the A-K of spades early, he unblocked his Q-J. West won the third round of spades and played a heart. Down one.

However, note the good play by declarer. If he waits till near the end of the hand to cash the A-K of spades, even someone on life support will probably realize what is happening and know to unblock.

UNBLOCKING TO DEFEND AGAINST AN ENDPLAY

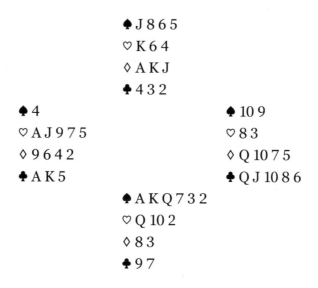

```
              ♠ J 8 6 5
              ♡ K 6 4
              ♢ A K J
              ♣ 4 3 2
♠ 4                           ♠ 10 9
♡ A J 9 7 5                   ♡ 8 3
♢ 9 6 4 2                     ♢ Q 10 7 5
♣ A K 5                       ♣ Q J 10 8 6
              ♠ A K Q 7 3 2
              ♡ Q 10 2
              ♢ 8 3
              ♣ 9 7
```

Contract: 4 ♠ (West overcalls hearts)
Opening Lead: ♣ Ace

West led the club ace, East played the queen. West led the club five, East won the ten and played the club queen. Declarer ruffed, drew trumps and played the A-K of diamonds. He ruffed a diamond and led the heart queen.

West was endplayed. A ruff/sluff or lead from his heart jack. Making four spades. "Did you think I put you in at trick two to lead another club?" asked West.

Question: How should the defenders avoid the endplay?

At the other table, play started the same, West underleading at trick two. But East did not think West wanted another club. He could have done that himself.
If East had returned the heart eight, West would have had a clear picture.

Even if the eight was a singleton, West would know to let dummy's heart king win, and that he would be getting two heart tricks later.
Down one, losing two clubs and two hearts.

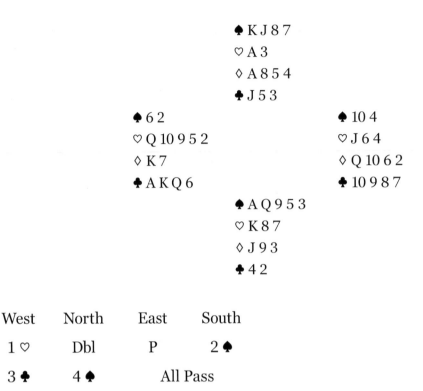

♠ K J 8 7
♡ A 3
◊ A 8 5 4
♣ J 5 3

♠ 6 2
♡ Q 10 9 5 2
◊ K 7
♣ A K Q 6

♠ 10 4
♡ J 6 4
◊ Q 10 6 2
♣ 10 9 8 7

♠ A Q 9 5 3
♡ K 8 7
◊ J 9 3
♣ 4 2

West	North	East	South
1 ♡	Dbl	P	2 ♠
3 ♣	4 ♠	All Pass	

Opening Lead: ♣ Ace

West led the top clubs and declarer ruffed the third round. Declarer cashed the diamond ace and drew trumps. He played the A-K of hearts and ruffed a heart.

When he played a low diamond from both hands, West won the king and was endplayed. The resultant ruff/sluff held declarer's diamond losers to one.

Question: Was there a way to defeat four spades?

The West player at the other table was more alert and unblocked his diamond king under the ace in an attempt to avoid the endplay. A valiant effort. The operation was a success, but the patient died.

When declarer led a low diamond from dummy, East had no good option. Win or duck the queen, declarer was only losing one more trick. Making four spades. Good try.

UNBLOCKING IN TRUMPS

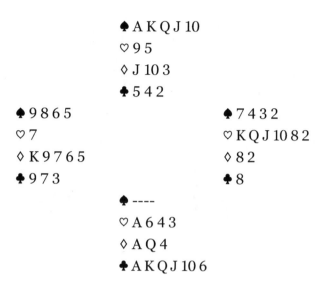

♠ A K Q J 10
♡ 9 5
◇ J 10 3
♣ 5 4 2

♠ 9 8 6 5   ♠ 7 4 3 2
♡ 7   ♡ K Q J 10 8 2
◇ K 9 7 6 5   ◇ 8 2
♣ 9 7 3   ♣ 8

♠ ----
♡ A 6 4 3
◇ A Q 4
♣ A K Q J 10 6

Contract: 6 ♣

Opening Lead: ♡ 7

Declarer won the opening lead. He cashed the A-K of trumps and exited with the trump six. West was endplayed. A diamond or spade lead allowed declarer to reach dummy.

Making six clubs.

Question: Could the defense have prevailed?

At the other table, play started the same, but when declarer played the A-K of trumps, West unblocked the ♣ 9 7. With no way to reach dummy, declarer had no play for the slam.

DEFENSE: LITTLE MORE OF THIS AND THAT

DON'T COVER - BLOCK THEIR SUIT

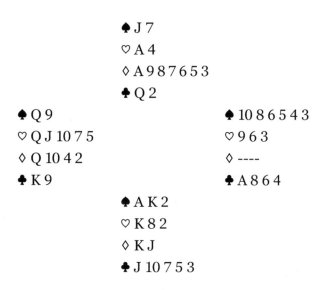

```
                    ♠ J 7
                    ♡ A 4
                    ◇ A 9 8 7 6 5 3
                    ♣ Q 2
      ♠ Q 9                          ♠ 10 8 6 5 4 3
      ♡ Q J 10 7 5                   ♡ 9 6 3
      ◇ Q 10 4 2                     ◇ ----
      ♣ K 9                          ♣ A 8 6 4
                    ♠ A K 2
                    ♡ K 8 2
                    ◇ K J
                    ♣ J 10 7 5 3
```

Contract: 3 NT
Opening Lead: ♡ Queen

Declarer won the opening lead in hand to preserve a dummy entry. He cashed the diamond king, East showing out, and led the diamond jack. "Oh no you don't," thought West, well trained in 'Rules' and 'covered an honor with an honor'.

"Thanks," thought South. He won the ace in dummy, conceded a diamond to West and had at least nine tricks. Making 3 NT.

Question: How did West defend at the other table?

'Rules' are guidelines in bridge. There are very few rules that are written in stone. Thinking takes priority. West simply ducked the diamond jack, blocking the suit.

Declarer could overtake and force out one of West's two high diamonds. But with only one dummy entry, declarer could never establish the diamond suit.

UNBLOCKING TO CREATE AN ENTRY FOR PARTNER

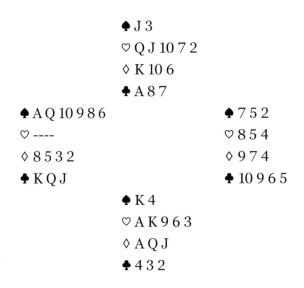

♠ J 3
♡ Q J 10 7 2
◇ K 10 6
♣ A 8 7

♠ A Q 10 9 8 6
♡ ----
◇ 8 5 3 2
♣ K Q J

♠ 7 5 2
♡ 8 5 4
◇ 9 7 4
♣ 10 9 6 5

♠ K 4
♡ A K 9 6 3
◇ A Q J
♣ 4 3 2

Contract: 4 ♡ (West overcalls spades)
Opening Lead: ♣ King

Declarer won the opening lead and drew trumps. He cashed three rounds of diamonds and led a club. West cashed two winning clubs and the spade ace.

Making four spades.

Question: How did the defense prevail at the other table?

To avoid being endplayed, West discarded his clubs when declarer was drawing trumps. When South played a club, East cashed two clubs and led a spade.

Down one.

INTENTIONALLY BLOCKING YOUR OWN SUIT

```
                    ♠ A K Q J 8
                    ♡ Q J
                    ◇ K Q 2
                    ♣ 10 4 2
     ♠ 7 6 3 2                          ♠ 9 4
     ♡ A 3                              ♡ 9 7 6 5
     ◇ 9 4                              ◇ J 10 8 5
     ♣ A 8 7 5 3                        ♣ K J 6
                    ♠ 10 5
                    ♡ K 10 8 4 2
                    ◇ A 7 6 3
                    ♣ Q 9
```

Contract: 3 NT
Opening Lead: ♣ 5

East won the king at trick one, declarer following with the nine. East made the 'book' return of the jack, high from a doubleton. West won, but the ten in dummy was high. At least he hadn't blocked the suit. Making 3 NT.

Question: How would a more 'thinking' defender handle this?

At the other table, East was less concerned about blocking the suit. He returned the six of clubs. West won and returned the club eight. East won the jack. The suit was blocked.

How to get to West? Just a guess? No, West's high eight of clubs was a suit preference signal. Between hearts and diamonds (if your partner thinks you want a spade, better get a new partner), West was telling East his entry was in hearts.

Down two.

BLOCKING YOUR OWN SUIT TO GET PARTNER ON LEAD

```
                    ♠ K 5
                    ♡ 10 4 2
                    ◊ K 7 4
                    ♣ Q 8 6 5 3
        ♠ Q 9 6 4 2              ♠ A J 10 8
        ♡ A Q 8                  ♡ 9 7 6
        ◊ J 8 6 5                ◊ 10 9 2
        ♣ 2                      ♣ J 9 4
                    ♠ 7 3
                    ♡ K J 5 3
                    ◊ A Q 3
                    ♣ A K 10 7
```

South	West	North	East
1 NT		All Pass	

Opening Lead: ♠ 4

Declarer hopefully played the king, East won the ace and continued with the spade jack. When that held, he played the ten, then the eight to West's queen.

West cashed the fifth spade. He had to cash his heart ace now to hold declarer to seven tricks, since declarer had eight minor tricks ready to cash.

"Too bad you didn't switch to a heart first," said West. "Why didn't you make me?" retorted East, looking very unhappy as he wrote - 90.

Question: What was East referring to? 1 NT went down at the other table.

The other West had watched the spade spots carefully. But he wanted a heart switch before cashing the spades. He overtook the spade ten with his queen and played a low spade to East's eight. The suit was blocked.

East wondered why his expert partner blocked the suit? He certainly knew better. So it had to be for a logical reason.

East played a heart, the only logical suit. Down one, the defense taking five spades and two hearts. East smiled as he wrote + 50.

DEFENDING WHEN THEIR SUIT IS BLOCKED

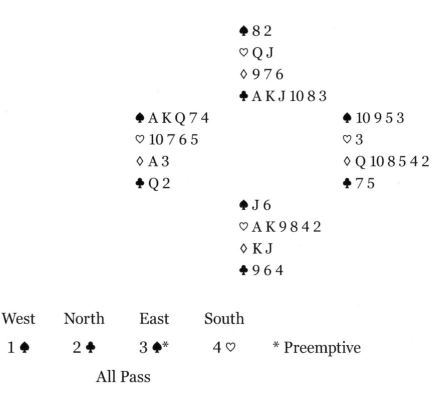

♠ 8 2
♥ Q J
♦ 9 7 6
♣ A K J 10 8 3

♠ A K Q 7 4   ♠ 10 9 5 3
♥ 10 7 6 5   ♥ 3
♦ A 3   ♦ Q 10 8 5 4 2
♣ Q 2   ♣ 7 5

♠ J 6
♥ A K 9 8 4 2
♦ K J
♣ 9 6 4

West	North	East	South	
1 ♠	2 ♣	3 ♠*	4 ♥	* Preemptive
	All Pass			

Opening Lead: ♠ Ace

West cashed two high spades and switched to a trump. Declarer cashed the other trump in dummy and led a diamond to his jack. West won and played another spade. Declarer ruffed, drew trumps and had the rest.

Making four hearts.

Question: Was there a better line of defense? That is a formidable second suit.

At the other table, West realized the trump suit was blocked. After two rounds of spades, he played ace and another diamond, removing declarer's entry to his hand.

After two rounds of trumps, declarer was locked in the dummy. West could ruff the third club and he could overruff the third diamond.

161

BLOCKING THE DECLARER'S SUIT

      ♠ A K Q 4
      ♡ Q 10
      ♦ A Q J
      ♣ 9 7 6 3

♠ J 10 8 6   ♠ 3 2
♡ J 3   ♡ K 9 8 7 6 5
♦ 9 3   ♦ K 7 2
♣ K Q J 10 4   ♣ 8 5

      ♠ 9 7 5
      ♡ A 4 2
      ♦ 10 8 6 5 4
      ♣ A 2

Contract: 3 NT
Opening Lead: ♣ King

Declarer won the second club and took a diamond finesse. East won and returned a spade. Declarer had nine tricks.

Three spades, one heart, four diamonds, and one club.

Question: At the other table, 3 NT went down. Do you see how?

The proper defense is the same principle as defending against a second suit type hand. Try to remove entries.

After winning the diamond king, East returned the heart king, removing declarer's only entry to his hand while the diamond suit was blocked.

Only eight tricks.

UNBLOCKING WHILE TAKING TRICKS IN DESPERATION

```
                    ♠ 10
                    ♡ A K Q J 2
                    ◊ A K Q 8
                    ♣ K 5 2
    ♠ A 9 8 7                       ♠ K J 3
    ♡ 10 7 5 4                      ♡ 9 6 3
    ◊ 6 4                           ◊ 10 7 5 2
    ♣ J 10 8                        ♣ A 9 7
                    ♠ Q 6 5 4 2
                    ♡ 8
                    ◊ J 9 3
                    ♣ Q 6 4 3
```

Contract: 3 NT (North opened 2 ♣)

Opening Lead: ♣ Jack

East won the club ace and switched to the spade three. The defense took two spade tricks. Declarer took the rest.

Question: What should East have considered before playing?

The other East saw five heart tricks and three diamond tricks in dummy, and knew declarer had the club queen. The only hope was spades. West didn't have five or he surely would have led one.

So declarer had five spades. East knew he needed to unblock, so he led the spade jack at trick two.

Four spade tricks and one club trick for the defense. Down one.

UNTANGLING YOUR TRICKS

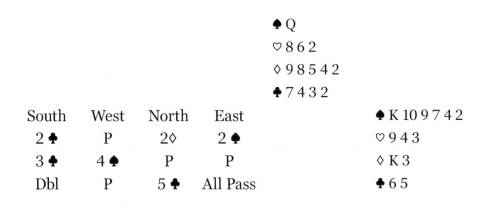

```
                                    ♠ Q
                                    ♡ 8 6 2
                                    ◊ 9 8 5 4 2
                                    ♣ 7 4 3 2
South    West    North    East              ♠ K 10 9 7 4 2
2 ♣      P       2◊       2 ♠               ♡ 9 4 3
3 ♣      4 ♠     P        P                 ◊ K 3
Dbl      P       5 ♣      All Pass          ♣ 6 5
```

Opening Lead: ♠ 5

Declarer wins the spade ace and leads the ace of clubs. West plays the jack, then discards the spade three on the next club. So declarer's lowest club is the eight and he has the singleton ace of spades. Declarer cannot reach dummy.

Declarer plays the ♡ A K Q and leads the ♦ 6 towards dummy. West plays the ten. East's play? One defender played low, one played high. Who was right?

```
                              ♠ Q
                              ♡ 8 6 2
                              ◊ 9 8 5 4 2
                              ♣ 7 4 3 2
      ♠ J 8 6 5 3                          ♠ K 10 9 7 4 2
      ♡ J 10 7 5                           ♡ 9 4 3
      ◊ A J 10                             ◊ K 3
      ♣ J                                  ♣ 6 5
                              ♠ A
                              ♡ A K Q
                              ◊ Q 7 6
                              ♣ A K Q 10 9 8
```

Did you play the diamond king? If you leave West on lead, he has two impossible choices. Cash the diamond ace crashing your king, or lead low to your king. Then you would have to give declarer a ruff/sluff.

UNBLOCKING TO HELP PARTNER
DO THE RIGHT THING

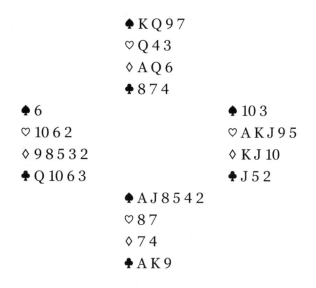

♠ K Q 9 7
♡ Q 4 3
♢ A Q 6
♣ 8 7 4

♠ 6
♡ 10 6 2
♢ 9 8 5 3 2
♣ Q 10 6 3

♠ 10 3
♡ A K J 9 5
♢ K J 10
♣ J 5 2

♠ A J 8 5 4 2
♡ 8 7
♢ 7 4
♣ A K 9

Contract: 4 ♠ (East overcalls hearts)
Opening Lead: ♡ 2

Declarer ruffed the third heart and drew trumps. He cashed the A-K of clubs and led a club. West played the ten, East had to play the jack. East was endplayed. A heart return was a ruff/sluff and a diamond return cost a diamond trick.

Making four spades.

"You could have helped me a little," complained West after misdefending.

Question: What was West referring to? How should the defense have gone?

At the other table, play went along the same lines. But both East and West were more attuned to what was going on. On the third club, West was planning to jump up with the queen, the Crocodile Coup, to swallow up his partner's card.

But East beat him to it by unblocking the club jack under the king to help out.

No endplay, down one.

DEFENDER CREATES AN EXTRA ENTRY FOR PARTNER

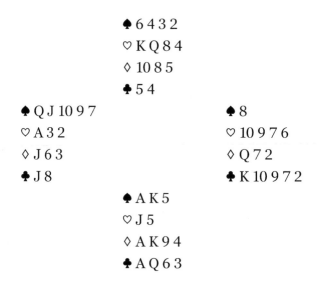

```
              ♠ 6 4 3 2
              ♡ K Q 8 4
              ◊ 10 8 5
              ♣ 5 4
♠ Q J 10 9 7              ♠ 8
♡ A 3 2                   ♡ 10 9 7 6
◊ J 6 3                   ◊ Q 7 2
♣ J 8                     ♣ K 10 9 7 2
              ♠ A K 5
              ♡ J 5
              ◊ A K 9 4
              ♣ A Q 6 3
```

Contract: 3 NT

Opening Lead: ♠ Queen

Declarer won the opening lead and cashed the A-K of diamonds. He led the heart jack. West won and continued spades. Declarer won, went to dummy with a heart and took a successful club finesse.

Then declarer led a diamond. East won, but when the diamonds were 3-3, declarer had nine tricks.

Question: At the other table, the defense prevailed. How did that happen?

West was thinking he might have ducked the first heart. But declarer could endplay East in diamonds to play a heart or club.

No, the winning play was by East, who unblocked the diamond queen under the A-K. This created an extra entry for West to run the spades, scoring three spades, one heart, and the diamond jack.

Printed in the United States
By Bookmasters